O
PITCH
MASTERING THE DEFENCE

BY
TOBY RIVERS

DCP

"Attack wins you games, but defence wins you titles."

Sir Alex Ferguson

Main Characters

Robin is an 11-year-old Australian boy with straight brown hair and a slightly shorter stature compared to his peers. Always wearing his favourite faded soccer jersey, he is determined and passionate about the sport. Throughout the season, Robin transforms from an eager learner into a dependable leader on the pitch. His vision and ability to anticipate plays make him an exceptional playmaker and defensive organiser. Robin's journey shows that soccer is about much more than winning—it's about resilience, teamwork, and personal growth.

Jake is a lively and confident midfielder known for his quick wit and even quicker feet. He's one of Robin's closest friends, always joking around and bringing energy to the team. Jake's bold personality translates to his playing style, where he thrives in high-pressure situations. Over the season, Jake learns to balance his attacking instincts with the discipline required for defensive duties, growing into a well-rounded player and a reliable teammate.

Alex is the team's hardworking central defender with a strong build and a determined personality. Known for his physicality and commitment, Alex sometimes struggles with managing his intensity on the field. After an incident where his overzealous tackle injures an opponent, Alex embarks on a journey of learning the importance of sportsmanship and controlled aggression in soccer. His growth inspires the team and underscores the values of respect and responsibility.

Ollie is a creative and fast-paced winger who loves taking risks and dazzling opponents with his footwork. With his blonde hair and infectious smile, Ollie is the team's morale booster, always finding a way to lighten the mood. While his attacking flair often puts him in the spotlight, Ollie learns the importance of tracking back and contributing defensively, making him a more complete player.

Tommy is the team's goalkeeper and a natural strategist with a sharp mind and exceptional reflexes. Off the field, he's a quiet, academic type who enjoys solving puzzles and tinkering with gadgets. On the field, Tommy becomes the backbone of the team, especially during critical moments, like saving penalties and leading defensive organisation. His calm demeanour under pressure inspires confidence in his teammates.

Contents

Previously with Robin On the Pitch

Robin's journey began with a dream—to play soccer like a pro. Through hard work, guidance from his mentor Mason, and support from his friends, Robin learned more than just dribbling, passing, and shooting. He discovered that teamwork, resilience, and respect are what make a true player. Along the way, Robin proved his skills and earned the chance to join a youth team. With his coach's guidance and the encouragement of his new teammates, Robin faced the exciting challenge of learning to play every position. From the steady central defender to the dynamic winger and the goal-scoring striker, Robin discovered the unique demands of each role and how they all contribute to the team.

A New Season, A New Challenge

Challenges on the field aren't obstacles; they're opportunities to rise stronger together.

The sun streamed through Robin's window, casting a warm glow across his room. It was the kind of morning that carried promise, and Robin could feel it in his bones. Today was the start of a new football season, and as much as he loved the summer break, he'd been itching to get back on the pitch.

The smell of toast and eggs wafted up from downstairs, pulling him from his thoughts. He quickly threw on a hoodie and jogged down to the kitchen, where his mum was busy at the stove, and his dad was seated at the table, engrossed in the sports section of the newspaper.

"Morning, champ," his dad greeted without looking up, a mug of coffee in his hand.

"Morning!" Robin replied, grabbing a plate and sitting down at his usual spot.

His mum turned with a smile, placing a steaming plate of eggs and toast in front of him. "First day back at training," she said. "Excited?"

Robin grinned. "Definitely. Coach said we're focusing on defence this season. He's got some big plans, I think."

His dad finally looked up, folding the newspaper neatly. "Defence, eh? That's where games are won. It's not as flashy as scoring, but it's just as important–maybe more."

"You've said that about ten times, Dad," Robin said, laughing.

"Well, it's true," his dad replied, smiling. "A good defence makes all the difference. You'll see."

His mum joined in, sitting across from him. "Just remember to have fun, Robin. It's about more than just winning, you know."

Robin nodded, taking a bite of toast. "I know, Mum. But I do want to get better this season. Coach said defence is about strategy and teamwork. I think it'll be fun."

After breakfast, Robin went upstairs to pack his gear. He grabbed his boots, shin guards, and jersey, carefully checking everything before stuffing it into his bag. On his desk sat the notebook he'd been using all summer–a collection of soccer tactics he'd been sketching out, inspired by his favourite players. He flipped through a few pages before tossing it in the bag as well. With his water bottle and a snack from his mum, he was ready to go.

Robin cycled to the pitch, the cool morning breeze whipping past him. The familiar sight of the green field came into view, already alive with the sounds of his teammates chatting and kicking balls around. He smiled. It felt good to be back.

He spotted Ollie, Jake, and Tommy near the centre circle, passing the ball between them. Robin hopped off his bike and jogged over.

"Look who finally decided to show up!" Ollie called out, grinning.

Robin rolled his eyes. "You wish I was late. I didn't want to embarrass you too early."

Jake laughed. "Right, Robin's been planning this big comeback all summer."

Tommy joined in. "Bet he's been sketching plays in that notebook of his, too."

Robin shrugged with a grin. "Maybe. You'll see soon enough."

The banter flowed easily as the friends caught up. Ollie bragged about a goal he'd scored in a beach football tournament over the summer, while Tommy talked about how he'd been working on his reflexes. Jake, ever the bookworm, shared a fact he'd learned about defensive strategies, which earned him a mix of groans and laughs.

"And you, Robin?" Ollie asked. "What have you been up to?"

"Practising my positioning," Robin said. "My dad's been going on and on about how important it is."

"Your dad and his 'defence wins games' motto?" Tommy joked. "Classic."

Just then, Coach Thompson arrived, his clipboard in hand and his signature no-nonsense expression softened by a rare smile. He blew his whistle, gathering the team around him.

"Alright, everyone," Coach began, looking around at the players. "First off, welcome back. I hope you all had a good summer because we've got a big season ahead of us."

He paused, letting the players settle. "Last season, we focused on learning the basics—skills and positions. You worked hard, and it showed. But this season, we're taking things up a notch. Our focus this time? Defence."

Robin's ears perked up. This was exactly what he'd been waiting to hear.

"Now, before you groan," Coach said, smiling slightly, "defence isn't just about blocking shots or tackling players. It's about strategy, discipline, and teamwork. It's the backbone of any great team."

The players nodded, a few exchanging curious looks. Coach continued, his tone serious but encouraging. "We'll start with the basics, but as the season progresses, we're going to dive into the art of defending. By the end, you'll understand how mastering the defence makes you better at every part of the game."

Robin felt a buzz of excitement. The way Coach spoke made it clear that this season would be different, more focused and challenging.

"Before we get started," Coach said, "I'd like to introduce two new players joining us this season."

He gestured toward two boys standing nearby. "This is Liam, a centre-back who loves organising the defence, and Ethan, a quick and versatile defender. Let's give them a warm welcome."

The team clapped and cheered as Liam and Ethan stepped forward with shy smiles. Robin exchanged a quick handshake with both, already looking forward to seeing them in action.

Coach Thompson blew his whistle again, signalling the start of a light training session. "Alright, let's ease into it today. There are no intense drills—just a warm-up to get the ball rolling, literally. Pair up, grab a ball, and start with some passing. Keep it simple."

Robin paired up with Ollie, who was already bouncing the ball off his foot with a grin. "Bet you I can make ten perfect passes before you mess one up," Ollie teased.

Robin smirked. "Dream on."

The two started passing, focusing on their technique. Around the pitch, laughter and chatter filled the air as the players reconnected on the field. The new players, Liam and Ethan, were quickly drawn into the mix, with teammates showing them the ropes and cracking jokes to make them feel at home.

After passing drills, Coach set up a small rondo game, with players taking turns in the middle trying to win the ball back. Robin found himself laughing as Jake tripped over his own feet in an attempt to intercept a slick pass from Tommy.

"Well, at least you're consistent, Jake!" Ollie shouted, earning a round of laughter.

The session ended with a few light sprints and stretches, leaving everyone feeling energised but not overworked. As the team huddled around Coach, he gave them a final word.

"Good start today, everyone. Tomorrow, we dive into the season plan, and I promise you, it's going to be challenging but worth it. Rest up, and I'll see you all fresh in the next training."

The players dispersed, some heading to their bikes, others lingering for a bit of banter. Robin stayed a moment longer, catching Liam and Ethan on their way out.

"You guys did great today," Robin said, offering a friendly smile. "Looking forward to seeing you in action."

"Thanks, Robin," Liam replied. "Same here. You guys seem like a good group."

As Robin walked his bike home, the cool evening breeze brushing against his face, he felt a sense of anticipation building. Tomorrow, the real work would begin. This season wasn't just about learning—it was about mastering the art of defence. And Robin was ready.

Tackling with Precision

A well-timed tackle can change the course of the game and define the heart of the defender.

The crisp morning breeze swept across the training pitch as Robin arrived, his soccer boots dangling from his shoulder. Today marked the first weekly session since the season began, and Coach Thompson had promised to focus on one of the most vital skills in soccer defence: tackling. Robin felt a surge of anticipation. Tackling wasn't just about stopping the opposition—it was a statement of control, a moment to turn defence into attack.

His teammates were already gathering on the pitch, chatting and warming up. The energy in the air was contagious, and Robin jogged over to join the group.

"Alright, lads!" Coach Thompson's familiar voice boomed across the field, instantly commanding attention. He stood at the centre of the pitch, holding a soccer ball.

His clipboard, a constant companion, was tucked under his arm. "Today, we're focusing on the art of tackling."

The players formed a semi-circle around Coach as he began his introduction. "Tackling is one of the most important tools in a defender's arsenal. But," he paused, looking each player in the eye, "it's not about diving in recklessly. A good tackle requires precision, control, and above all, timing."

Robin listened intently, his mind racing with thoughts of past games where well-timed tackles had changed the course of play. He couldn't wait to sharpen his skills.

Coach continued, motioning for Ethan to step forward as his demonstration partner. "We'll start with the basics. First up: the standing tackle. This is your go-to move when you're face-to-face with an opponent and need to take the ball cleanly."

Ethan began dribbling slowly toward Coach. With a calculated step, Coach lunged forward, hooking the ball with his foot and maintaining perfect balance. "Key points," he said, straightening up. "Stay balanced, keep your eyes on the ball, and wait for the attacker to commit before you make your move. Timing is everything."

Next, he moved on to the sliding tackle. Placing a cone and a ball a few feet apart, Coach sprinted toward them and executed a textbook slide, knocking the ball away cleanly without touching the cone. "This one is riskier," he explained, brushing off his knees. "Only use it when absolutely necessary—like when the opposition is about to score. It's high-risk, high-reward, so make sure you time it perfectly."

Finally, Coach demonstrated the block tackle. "This one is all about strength and positioning," he said, standing firm as Ethan approached. As Ethan tried to shoot, Coach planted himself in front of the ball, blocking it with his foot and sending it out of play. "When you can't dispossess them, stopping the shot is just as important."

The team split into pairs for the first drill: 1v1 standing tackles. Each defender had to stop their partner from dribbling past them. Robin was paired with Ethan, who had lightning-quick feet. At first, Robin struggled to judge the timing. Twice, Ethan slipped past him with a cheeky grin.

"Patience, Robin!" Coach called from the sideline. "Don't dive in too early. Let Ethan make the first move."

Taking a deep breath, Robin refocused. He watched Ethan closely, waiting for the moment he shifted his weight to make a move. When Ethan tried to cut to the left, Robin stepped in, hooked the ball away, and stood his ground.

"Yes, Robin! That's the way!" Coach shouted, and Robin couldn't help but smile. He passed the ball back to Ethan, ready for another round.

Next, they moved to the sliding tackle drill. Cones were arranged to simulate attackers, and each player took turns sliding to knock the ball away while keeping the cones untouched. Robin watched as Ollie, who was more used to flashy footwork than defensive plays, sent both the ball and the cone flying in his first attempt. The team erupted into laughter, even Ollie, who threw his hands up in mock defeat.

When it was Robin's turn, he approached the ball cautiously. He remembered Coach's advice: wait until the last possible moment. Dropping into a controlled slide, he connected cleanly with the ball, sending it rolling out of bounds while the cone remained upright.

"Well done, Robin!" Coach said with a nod. "Controlled, precise—exactly what we need."

The final drill focused on block tackles. Players took turns defending against Tommy, their goalkeeper, who was acting as a striker for the day. Tommy's shots were fierce and fast, challenging even the most confident defenders. Robin found this exercise particularly tough—more than once, Tommy managed to power through his attempts to block.

But Robin wasn't one to back down. On his next attempt, he braced himself as Tommy charged forward. Watching Tommy's movement closely, Robin stepped into the ball's path, planting his feet and deflecting the shot wide.

"Brilliant block!" Coach shouted, clapping his hands. "That's how you stand your ground!"

As the session came to a close, Coach Thompson gathered the team for a final debrief. "Great work today, everyone. Tackling isn't just about stopping the ball—it's about reading the game, staying calm, and making smart decisions under pressure."

He looked around at the group, his expression serious but encouraging. "Remember, these skills take time to master. Keep practising, keep pushing yourselves, and these techniques will become second nature."

Robin felt a sense of accomplishment as he walked off the pitch with Ethan and Ollie. Today's session had been a mix of challenges and victories, and it left him eager for the next practice. Tackling, he realised, was as much about patience and strategy as it was about physical skill.

As he slung his bag over his shoulder and headed home, Robin couldn't help but feel that he was beginning to understand the true art of defending.

Testing the Defence - A Friendly Match Challenge

Challenges on the field aren't obstacles; they're opportunities to rise stronger together.

The air buzzed with excitement as Robin and his teammates arrived at the soccer field for their first friendly match of the season. The opposing team, known for their quick attacks and strong coordination, was a local favourite, which made the challenge even more thrilling. Robin adjusted the strap of his gear bag, feeling a mix of nerves and anticipation.

Coach Thompson stood at the entrance of the field, clipboard in hand, waiting for the team to gather around. His usual calm demeanour was laced with just a hint of intensity. "Alright, everyone," he began, looking at each of them, "this is our chance to put everything we've been working on into practice. This game isn't about the score—it's about showing what you've learned, especially in defence. Remember, tackling isn't just about taking the ball. It's about timing, patience, and decision-making. Stick to your roles, and trust each other out there."

The players nodded, though there was an unmistakable buzz of curiosity. Coach hadn't assigned them specific positions yet, and Robin wondered where he would be playing.

As if reading their minds, Coach added, "Robin, Ethan, you'll be our central defenders for today. I want the two of you to work as a unit. Cover each other, communicate constantly, and make sure to stay organised. Ollie, you'll play on the left wing, and Alex will cover the right flank. Everyone else, stick to your usual roles. Let's see how you all handle this."

Robin felt a surge of responsibility. Playing as a central defender alongside Ethan was a challenge he hadn't faced much before. But he also felt confident, knowing they'd trained hard for moments like this.

The whistle blew, and the game kicked off with a burst of energy. From the start, the opposition pressed hard, testing the team's composure and organisation. Robin found himself in the thick of it, constantly scanning the field and communicating with Ethan to keep their line intact. The opposing midfielders were quick, zipping passes between each other and looking for gaps to exploit.

Within the first few minutes, Robin was forced into action. One of their forwards charged toward him with the ball, trying to dribble past. Robin remembered Coach

Thompson's advice: Stay calm, watch their movements, and wait for the right moment. As the forward made a move to his left, Robin stepped in with a clean standing tackle, dispossessing him and quickly passing the ball forward to Ollie.

"Nice one, Robin!" Ethan called as he moved into position to cover.

The game continued at a relentless pace. The opposition, undeterred by Robin's tackle, regrouped and began attacking down the wings. Ollie, playing on the left, attempted a sliding tackle near the sideline but mistimed it, clipping the attacker's leg and earning a free kick for the other team.

"Unlucky, Ollie!" Coach Thompson shouted from the sideline. "Stay patient and time it better next time."

Ollie grimaced but gave a thumbs-up. "I'll get it right," he muttered to Robin as they jogged back into position.

Robin glanced at him. "You will. Just don't rush it."

The opposition's pressure began to mount as they exploited the team's defensive gaps. Ethan, playing alongside Robin, over-committed to an attacker, leaving space for their star striker to charge through. Robin sprinted back, positioning himself between the striker and the goal. The striker wound up for a shot, but Robin anticipated it, stepping in with a perfectly timed block tackle that sent the ball spinning away.

"Great block, Robin!" Ethan shouted, rushing to clear the ball further downfield. Robin felt a surge of confidence as he jogged back into position, exchanging a quick nod with Ethan.

The team managed to hold the opposition off until halftime, but it hadn't been easy. In the changing room, Coach Thompson addressed the team. "You've done well to stay organised, but we're still rushing some of our decisions. Ollie, your sliding tackle needs work. Don't dive in too early—wait until the ball is in your range. Ethan, watch your positioning. You're leaving gaps that they're exploiting. And Robin, excellent work so far. Keep up that composure."

The team nodded, absorbing Coach's feedback. Ollie leaned over to Robin. "I'll get that slide right. Just wait and see."

"I know you will," Robin replied with a grin.

The second half began with renewed determination. Robin could feel the shift in the team's energy. They communicated more effectively, shouting instructions and covering each other's positions. When the opposition launched another attack, Ollie redeemed himself with a clean sliding tackle that sent the ball out for a throw-in. The team cheered, and even Coach Thompson clapped from the sideline.

The opposition continued to push, but the team's improved coordination kept them at bay. Robin found himself intercepting passes and initiating counterattacks, his confidence growing with each successful play. Ethan, too, stepped up, making crucial tackles and ensuring the defence held strong.

In the final minutes of the game, the opposition launched a last-ditch attack. Their star striker received a through-ball and sprinted toward the goal, only to be met by Robin, who executed a decisive block tackle, stopping the play in its tracks. The crowd, mostly parents and local supporters, erupted into applause.

As the final whistle blew, the game ended in a draw, but the result didn't matter. The team had shown resilience and growth, and Coach Thompson was visibly pleased.

Gathering the players together, he said, "That was a solid performance. You applied what we've been practising, and it showed. We still have areas to improve, but this was a step in the right direction. Well done."

Robin felt a sense of pride as he high-fived his teammates. The match had been a challenge, but it had also been an opportunity to put their skills to the test. As they packed up their gear, Ethan turned to Robin.

"You were on fire out there. That block tackle at the end was class."

"Thanks," Robin said, slinging his bag over his shoulder. "But we all did our part. Next game, we'll be even better."

As they left the pitch, Robin couldn't help but feel excited for what lay ahead. The season was just beginning, and he knew there was still so much to learn and accomplish.

Mastering Marking

Marking isn't just about staying close—it's about staying smart and one step ahead·

The team gathered at the training pitch early on a bright morning, the energy from their recent friendly game still lingering in the air. Robin could hear the excited chatter among his teammates as they laced up their boots, eager to see what Coach Thompson had planned for the session. As usual, Coach stood in the centre of the field, clipboard in hand and a knowing smile on his face.

"All right, team," Coach began, his voice carrying across the pitch, "today, we're diving into something every defender needs to master—marking. Whether you're defending against the fastest winger or the trickiest playmaker, good marking can make the difference between winning and losing."

Robin straightened, his interest piqued. He had heard of marking before but hadn't spent much time focused solely on it. Standing nearby, Ollie gave him a nudge. "This should be interesting," he whispered.

Coach continued, setting the scene. "Marking is all about staying close to your opponent, tracking their movement, and ensuring they don't have the time or space to do anything dangerous. Today, we'll start with man-to-man marking—the most fundamental type."

Coach walked the players through the key principles of man-to-man marking, using simple explanations to keep things clear. He demonstrated with Ethan, one of the midfielders, how to position yourself between the ball and the opponent.

"First rule," Coach said, pointing to Ethan's hips, "always watch the player, not the ball. The ball might move unpredictably, but the player's hips will tell you where they're going."

Coach stepped back, continuing his explanation. "Second rule: stay close, but not too close. You want to be close enough to apply pressure but not so tight that you get spun around or lose sight of the ball."

Robin listened carefully, committing the tips to memory. These little details, he realised, could make a huge difference in how effectively he defended.

Coach Thompson clapped his hands. "Enough talk— time to get moving. Let's start with a simple drill to work on your positioning and reactions."

The players paired up, with one acting as the attacker and the other as the defender. Robin was paired with

Ethan. The goal was simple: the attacker would move around within a designated area, trying to lose their marker, while the defender's job was to stay as close as possible without committing a foul.

Robin crouched slightly, watching Ethan's every move. Ethan darted left, then right, trying to shake him off, but Robin stayed focused, adjusting his position with each change in direction. At first, he was a little too eager, getting too close and losing balance. But as the drill progressed, he found the right rhythm, staying light on his feet and keeping Ethan in his sight at all times.

"Good, Robin! That's it—don't rush, just stay close and anticipate the movement," Coach called out.

Next, Coach set up a larger drill. Two lines of players stood on either side of the pitch. One line was the attackers, and the other was the defenders. The attackers would receive a pass from Coach and try to advance toward the goal, while the defenders had to mark them and either intercept the ball or force them wide.

When Robin's turn came, he squared off against Ollie. Coach sent a low pass toward Ollie, who controlled it smoothly and started to advance. Robin stayed close, mirroring his every step. As Ollie tried to cut inside, Robin anticipated the move, stepping in to block his path and forcing him to turn back.

"Well played, Robin," Ollie said with a grin as the whistle blew. "You're getting better at reading the game."

For the final drill of the session, Coach introduced a small-sided game. Two teams faced off in a half-pitch setup, with defenders tasked specifically with marking their assigned opponents. Robin was assigned to mark Alex, a quick-footed forward who had a knack for slipping past defenders.

The game was fast-paced, with the midfielders constantly switching the play and forcing the defenders to stay alert. Robin stayed tight to Alex, using everything he had learned in the earlier drills. When Alex tried to sprint down the wing, Robin matched his pace, forcing him to the sideline and cutting off his options. When Alex tried to drop back and receive the ball, Robin was right there, preventing him from turning.

"Great work, Robin!" Coach called out as the game ended. "You're starting to understand how to stay composed under pressure."

Robin wiped the sweat from his brow, feeling a mix of exhaustion and pride. The drills had been challenging, but he could already see the improvement in his ability to track and contain opponents. As he packed up his gear, he couldn't help but feel excited for the next session. This was just the beginning, and he was eager to see how far he could go.

The players huddled together, catching their breath after the fast-paced, small-sided game. Coach Thompson stood at the centre of the group, his expression thoughtful. "Alright," he began, "now that we've worked on man-to-man marking, it's time to add a bit of complexity. We're going to shift our focus to zonal marking."

Robin raised an eyebrow, intrigued. He had heard about zonal marking but didn't fully understand how it differed from man-to-man marking. Coach seemed to notice the puzzled expressions on a few faces and quickly explained.

"Zonal marking," Coach began, "is about defending an area rather than a specific player. Instead of following your opponent all over the pitch, you focus on protecting your assigned zone and dealing with any threats that enter it. This is especially important during set pieces, like corners or free-kicks."

The team nodded, eager to dive into the next set of drills. Coach wasted no time setting up the next activity.

Coach laid out cones to mark specific zones in the penalty area. The defenders were assigned to these zones, while attackers were tasked with making runs into the box to receive a cross. The defenders' goal was to maintain their position and clear the ball when it entered their zone.

Robin was placed in a central zone, right in front of the goal. He watched as the first wave of attackers made their moves, darting in and out of the zones to try and create confusion. A high cross came sailing into the box, and Robin sprang into action, leaping to head the ball clear.

"Great clearance, Robin!" Coach shouted. "But remember, don't drift out of your zone. Trust your teammates to cover theirs."

The drill continued, with attackers trying different types of runs and crosses. Robin quickly realised how important communication was in zonal marking. He began calling out to his teammates, letting them know when an attacker was entering their zone or when he was stepping up to challenge the ball.

Next, Coach introduced a scenario that mimicked a corner kick. The defenders lined up in their zones while attackers prepared to make runs from the edge of the box. Coach emphasised the importance of staying disciplined and not getting drawn out of position.

Robin positioned himself near the penalty spot, scanning the area and keeping an eye on the attackers. When the corner was delivered, a towering attacker tried to run into his zone to challenge for the ball. Robin held his ground, jumping at the perfect moment to head the ball away.

"Good work, Robin!" Coach called out. "That's how you stay disciplined. Don't let the attacker dictate your movement—control your zone."

The team rotated through the drill, with defenders taking turns in different zones. Robin found himself growing more confident with each repetition, understanding how to balance awareness of his zone with the movements of his teammates.

For the final drill of the session, Coach set up a hybrid scenario that combined man-to-man and zonal marking. The attackers were instructed to overload certain areas, forcing the defenders to communicate and decide when to stick to their man and when to hand them off to a teammate.

Robin was tasked with marking Ethan, who was known for his clever movement. As Ethan tried to move into another defender's zone, Robin called out, "Switch!" The transition was seamless, with the other defender picking up Ethan while Robin stayed in his zone to cover a new attacker.

"Perfect communication!" Coach shouted. "That's what I want to see—working together as a unit."

As the sun began to dip lower in the sky, Coach Thompson called the team together one last time. The players were tired but energised by the day's work.

"Today, you've all taken big steps forward," Coach said, his voice filled with pride. "Marking—whether it's man-to-man or zonal—is all about discipline, communication, and awareness. You showed me today that you're capable of mastering these skills. Keep practising, and these techniques will become second nature."

Robin wiped the sweat from his face, feeling both exhausted and accomplished. The drills had been intense, but he could see the progress he and his teammates had made. As they packed up their gear, Robin exchanged a grin with Ollie. They had learned a lot today, and he knew it would make them stronger in the games to come.

Walking off the pitch, Robin felt a renewed sense of determination. This was just the start of their journey to mastering the defence, and he couldn't wait to see what challenges the next training session would bring.

The Art of Reading the Game

Anticipation is the art of seeing what's coming and having the courage to act first.

The morning air was crisp, carrying a promise of excitement as Robin arrived at the pitch. His teammates were already gathering, the chatter of excitement filling the space. They all knew today's session was about something crucial: learning to anticipate and intercept—skills that could turn the tide of any match.

Coach Thompson called the team together as they huddled around him. His tone was encouraging but focused. "Good morning, everyone. Today, we're working on a skill that separates good defenders from great ones. Interception and anticipation are what give you the edge. It's not just about reacting; it's about reading the game, seeing the play before it happens."

Robin stood beside Dylan and Alex, nodding in agreement. Dylan, the dependable defensive back, nudged Robin. "Think you're good at mind-reading, Robin?" he teased with a grin.

Robin chuckled. "Maybe after this session."

Coach continued, gesturing towards the field where cones and grids had been set up. "We're going to focus on reading your opponent. Watch their body language, their positioning, even the slightest glance. Those details will tell you where the ball is going."

The session began with a warm-up designed to sharpen both their bodies and minds. The players lined up for agility ladders, weaving their feet quickly through the rungs while keeping their heads up.

"Eyes up, Robin!" Coach called. "You can't anticipate if you're staring at your own feet."

Robin laughed, narrowly avoiding a stumble. Dylan, two lanes over, smirked. "Careful, mate. If you trip here, how are you going to stop a through ball?"

Next, they moved on to short sprints, reacting to Coach's calls. If he shouted "left," they darted to the nearest cone in that direction. The fast-paced nature of the drill already had everyone sweating, but the competitive spirit lightened the atmosphere.

When Coach called a sudden "stop," Ollie, the quick-witted winger, slid dramatically to a halt. "How was that for anticipation?" he joked, drawing laughter from the group.

For the first main drill, the team was divided into attackers and defenders in a small grid. The attackers' goal was to complete quick passes, while the defenders focused on intercepting.

Robin found himself paired with Dylan against Alex and Ollie, who relished their attacking roles. "Ready to watch us dance circles around you?" Ollie taunted, his grin infectious.

Robin raised an eyebrow. "We'll see who's dancing when we take the ball."

Coach observed as the drill began. Robin immediately noticed Ollie's subtle movements—how his body turned slightly before passing. Robin stepped into the anticipated passing lane, cutting off a sharp pass to Alex and earning a rare scowl from Ollie.

"Not bad," Ollie muttered. "But I'll get you next time."

Dylan managed another interception, reading Alex's hesitation as he tried to switch play. "They're good, but we're better," Dylan said with a wink.

The next drill emphasised positioning. Players were arranged in a larger setup, simulating game scenarios where defenders needed to cover passing options while maintaining their awareness of attackers.

Coach blew the whistle, and Robin found himself matched against Alex once more. Alex was trying to find Ollie, who was running into space. Robin positioned himself just right, making it difficult for Alex to pass without risking a turnover.

"Don't make it easy for them!" Coach shouted. "Force them to rethink their options."

Alex, feeling the pressure, attempted a lofted pass. Robin timed his jump perfectly, heading the ball away. "Gotcha!" he called out, unable to resist teasing Alex.

Nearby, Dylan was in a similar battle with Ollie. "You've got to do better than that," Dylan taunted as he intercepted a ground pass.

Ollie smirked. "Oh, just wait. I'm warming up."

To wrap up the session, Coach set up a small-sided game. The attackers were instructed to move the ball quickly, while the defenders focused on intercepting and launching counterattacks.

Robin and Dylan took up positions as central defenders, working together to shut down Ollie's clever passing attempts. Robin spotted Ollie's intent to play a through ball and stepped forward just in time, cutting it off cleanly.

"Nice one, Robin!" Dylan called, clapping him on the back.

The game continued with intensity, but there were light-hearted moments too. At one point, Ollie attempted a no-look pass that ended up going straight to Dylan. "Fancy, but useless," Dylan said with a laugh, passing the ball forward to Alex, who launched a counterattack.

By the end of the game, both teams were exhausted but buzzing with energy. The defenders intercepted more passes than Coach expected, and the attackers gained valuable experience in dealing with tight marking.

Coach gathered everyone for a final talk. "Great work today, team. Interception is a skill that requires focus, awareness, and positioning, but most of all, it requires patience. You won't win every ball, but when you do, it can change the game."

As they cooled down, Robin and Ollie exchanged a handshake. "Good defending today," Ollie said grudgingly. "But don't get too comfortable—I'll get you next time."

Robin grinned. "Bring it on."

The camaraderie was evident as the team packed up, joking and reliving the day's highlights. Robin felt a renewed sense of confidence. The drills had been tough, but they had also been fun, and he knew that mastering interception and anticipation would make a huge difference in the games to come.

The Interception Challenge

True strength lies in the moments we adapt, react, and stand united under pressure.

The morning sun cast a golden glow over the pitch as Robin arrived, his backpack slung over one shoulder and a bottle of water in hand. The familiar chatter of his teammates filled the air, and he smiled as he spotted Dylan and Ollie near the goalposts, playfully kicking a ball back and forth.

"Looks like someone's ready to show off today," Robin called out, jogging toward them.

"Ready to intercept every pass you try to make," Dylan shot back with a grin. "I've been practising my jumps."

Ollie laughed. "Don't get too confident, Dylan. You've got to catch me first."

Robin chuckled, dropping his bag near the sidelines. The team's camaraderie always put him at ease, even on challenging days. As the rest of the team arrived, Coach Thompson walked onto the field, clipboard in hand and a knowing look on his face.

"Alright, team, gather up!" Coach called out, and the players quickly formed a semi-circle around him.

"I've got something special for you today," he began, scanning their curious faces. "We've got a friendly game lined up. But there's a twist—it's all about interceptions. I want to see how well you can read the game, anticipate passes, and disrupt the opposition's play."

A murmur of excitement rippled through the group. Robin felt a mix of anticipation and nerves. Interceptions were tricky—they required sharp instincts and quick decisions.

"There's one more thing," Coach added with a sly grin. "I'm not telling you which positions you'll play. You'll find out when the game starts. Stay adaptable."

Robin exchanged glances with Dylan, who whispered, "I bet he's putting me in midfield just to mess with me."

"You'll survive," Robin replied with a smirk. "Probably."

As the whistle blew, Robin found himself in a familiar spot—centre-back alongside Dylan. Coach had made his point clear: this game would test their ability to stay focused and anticipate the opposition's moves.

The opposing team wasted no time asserting themselves. Their playmaker, a nimble midfielder with sharp vision, began dictating the game, sending quick, precise passes that tested Robin and Dylan's defensive line.

Early on, Robin saw a chance to intercept a pass intended for their striker. He stepped forward, confident he could reach it, but misjudged the speed of the ball. The striker latched onto it and fired a shot at goal. Tommy reacted brilliantly, diving low to his right and parrying the ball away.

"Come on, Robin!" Tommy called, brushing dirt off his gloves. "We can't let them get through that easily!"

Robin raised a hand in acknowledgement. "My bad, Tommy. I'll get the next one."

A few minutes later, Dylan found himself in a similar situation. A long ball was launched toward the opposition's winger, and Dylan, determined to cut it off, leapt for the interception. But he mistimed his jump, and the winger sped past him. Robin sprinted to cover, forcing the winger wide before he could deliver a dangerous cross.

As the play reset, Dylan jogged over, shaking his head. "That was terrible. My timing was all over the place."

"You're not alone," Robin said with a grin. "We've both got some work to do."

The coach called the team over during the break, and his expression was calm but firm. "Alright, it's not perfect, but I see progress. Robin, Dylan, you're starting to read their playmaker better, but you're committing too early. Stay patient. Let them make the first move."

He turned to the midfielders. "Alex, you've got to close down that playmaker faster. Force him into rushed decisions. And Ollie, when we counter, I want you looking for those wide spaces. That's where we'll catch them off guard."

Robin glanced at Alex, who nodded. "Got it, Coach. I'll stay tighter."

The team returned to the pitch with renewed focus. Robin and Dylan began coordinating their movements more effectively, using subtle signals to decide who would step forward and who would hold back. Early in the half, Robin saw an opportunity. The opposition's playmaker attempted a through-ball to their striker, but Robin read the pass and stepped in just in time to intercept it.

"Nice one, Robin!" Dylan shouted as Robin quickly played the ball to Alex, who launched a counterattack.

Alex, determined to redeem himself, battled fiercely in midfield, intercepting a risky diagonal pass and threading the ball through to Ollie on the wing. Ollie's pace was electric as he darted past two defenders, delivering a cross that just missed its mark.

"Close one, Ollie!" Robin called, giving him a thumbs-up.

"Next time, it's going in!" Ollie replied with a wink.

The turning point came when Dylan made a crucial interception, cutting out a long ball that had bypassed the midfield. He calmly passed it to Robin, who found Alex in space. Alex spotted Ollie making a run and sent a perfectly weighted pass his way. Ollie controlled it with ease and whipped the ball into the box. This time, their striker connected, sending it soaring into the net.

"Goal!" Tommy yelled from the back, pumping his fists in celebration.

As the whistle blew, the team gathered on the pitch, their spirits high despite the challenges they had faced.

"That's how you learn," Coach Thompson said, addressing the group. "Mistakes happen, but it's about how you adapt. Robin, Dylan, Alex—great improvement in reading the game. And Ollie, excellent work on the counter."

Robin felt a sense of pride as Coach's words sank in. The game had tested them, but it had also shown how much they were growing as a team. Laughing and joking with his teammates as they walked off the pitch, Robin knew this was only the beginning of their journey.

High Press and Counter-Pressing

The power of pressing lies in teamwork and the trust that every move counts.

The morning sun was bright, casting long shadows across the soccer pitch as Robin and his friends gathered for another weekly training session. The team had grown closer over the past few weeks, and despite the demanding training schedule, the atmosphere was filled with laughter and camaraderie.

"Do you think today's session will be as intense as last week?" Dylan asked, stretching his legs.

"I hope not," Alex replied with a grin. "My legs are still sore from all those marking drills."

Robin, lacing up his boots, smiled at his friends. "Whatever it is, let's just stay focused. You know how Coach loves to surprise us."

Moments later, Coach Thompson walked onto the pitch with his usual air of authority, clipboard in hand. "Alright, everyone, bring it in!" he called. "Today, we're focusing on a crucial aspect of defending and attacking—high pressing and counter-pressing."

The players gathered around, eager to hear what was in store.

Coach Thompson began with a short lecture. "High pressing," he explained, "is when we apply intense pressure on the opposition in their half of the pitch, forcing them to make mistakes and win the ball back quickly. It's not just about running at the ball—it's about reading the game, working as a team, and knowing when to press and when to hold back."

"And counter-pressing?" Ollie asked.

"Counter-pressing," Coach replied, "happens the moment we lose possession. Instead of falling back, we immediately pressure the opposition to regain the ball before they can start an attack. This tactic is all about speed, anticipation, and teamwork."

Robin nodded, his mind already racing with ideas. The concept sounded simple enough, but he knew there was more to it than met the eye.

Coach divided the pitch into smaller zones, using cones to mark each area. Each zone had two defenders and two attackers.

"Here's how it works," Coach explained. "The attackers will move the ball around their zone while the defenders work together to press them and win back possession.

The goal is not just to win the ball but to cut off passing options and force mistakes."

Robin was paired with Dylan, and they faced off against Ollie and Alex. As the drill began, Ollie and Alex passed the ball quickly, trying to outmanoeuvre the press. Robin and Dylan worked together, closing down space and anticipating their next moves.

"Don't just chase the ball!" Coach called. "Think ahead. Robin, if Dylan presses, you need to block the passing lane. Force them into a mistake."

The advice paid off. Dylan pressured Ollie, and Robin moved to intercept the pass to Alex, successfully winning the ball.

"Great work, boys!" Coach said. "That's the key to high pressing–working as a unit, not individuals."

After a quick water break, Coach introduced the next drill. "Now we'll focus on counter-pressing. The moment you lose the ball, you have five seconds to win it back. This drill will help you improve your reaction time and teamwork."

Coach set up a 5v5 game on a small pitch. The rule was simple: if a team lost possession, they had to immediately counter-press to regain control.

As the drill began, Robin's team lost the ball to Ollie's side. Without hesitation, Robin charged toward the player with the ball while Dylan and Alex moved to block passing options. The pressure was too much for Ollie's team, and they lost the ball within seconds.

"That's how you do it!" Coach shouted. "Immediate pressure cut off options and force them to make mistakes."

The drill was repeated several times, and the players began to understand the nuances of counter-pressing. Dylan, who had struggled earlier, found his rhythm and intercepted a pass, earning cheers from his teammates.

"Nice one, Dylan!" Robin said, giving him a high five.

To finish the session, Coach set up a small-sided game with a pressing focus. "This time," he said, "both teams will use high pressing. I'll be watching how well you communicate and work together."

The game started at a blistering pace. Robin's team pressed high, forcing the opposition to play long balls. At one point, Robin intercepted a pass and set up Alex for a goal.

"Brilliant press, Robin!" Coach called. "That's exactly what I want to see."

The opposition fought back, using quick passes to evade the press. Ollie managed to slip through the defence and score, earning applause from both teams.

Throughout the drills, Coach emphasised the importance of communication and anticipation. "Pressing isn't just about running hard," he said. "It's about thinking smart. Talk to each other, read the game, and stay disciplined."

As the session wound down, the players gathered for a final huddle. "Great work today," Coach said. "High pressing and counter-pressing are demanding tactics, but when done right, they can turn defence into attack in an instant. Remember, it's not just about effort–it's about strategy and teamwork."

The training ended with light-hearted banter among the players. Alex teased Dylan about his initial hesitation, while Tommy joked about being "the one-man press" in goal.

Robin, feeling a mix of exhaustion and accomplishment, joined his friends as they walked off the pitch. "That was tough," he said, "but I can see why it's so important. Pressing can really change a game."

"Yeah," Ollie agreed. "But next time, I'm breaking through your press, Robin. Just wait and see."

Robin laughed. "We'll see about that."

As the team headed home, Robin couldn't help but feel grateful for the lessons they were learning–not just about soccer but about resilience, strategy, and the power of working together.

Team Bonding Over Dinner

True teams aren't just built on the pitch; they're built in the bonds of friendship.

The warm glow of the local restaurant spilt onto the street as Robin approached with his parents. The faint hum of conversation and the clinking of glasses greeted them as they stepped inside. It wasn't the usual setting for the team, but tonight was special. The long table at the centre of the restaurant was already buzzing with laughter and chatter as his teammates gathered for their first bonding dinner of the season.

Robin spotted Dylan and Alex at one end of the table, laughing over something Ollie had just said. Dylan waved him over, and Robin quickly joined them, exchanging quick hellos with everyone. The atmosphere was light and easy, a stark contrast to the intensity of the pitch.

"Hey, Robin," Ollie called out, grinning as he shoved a breadstick into his mouth. "Don't sit too close to Dylan. He's still sore from that tackle you gave him last week."

Dylan rolled his eyes, smirking. "At least I wasn't the one getting nutmegged every five minutes in the drills."

"Fair point," Ollie shot back, grinning as the table erupted into laughter.

Robin shook his head, chuckling. "I'll try to keep my nutmegs to a minimum next time."

As more food arrived, the conversation shifted to lighter topics. Plates of pasta, salads, and grilled chicken were passed around as the kids began sharing bits of their lives outside of soccer.

"So, Robin," Alex said, leaning over the table, "other than nutmegging poor Dylan, what have you been up to?"

Robin smiled, setting his fork down. "Honestly, reading a lot. I always try to squeeze in a chapter or two before practice. It helps me stay focused."

"Reading?" Ollie piped up, a mock look of shock on his face. "What is this, the 1800s?"

The table laughed, and Robin shrugged good-naturedly. "It's better than whatever you're doing, Hollywood."

"Hollywood?" Dylan asked, raising an eyebrow.

"Yeah, did you know Ollie's been taking drama classes?" Robin said, grinning. "He's already practising his award speeches."

"Guilty," Ollie admitted, raising his hands dramatically. "But hey, when I'm a famous actor, don't come asking for tickets to my shows."

"You'll be lucky if you get cast as a tree," Dylan teased, earning another round of laughter.

Alex chimed in next. "I've been working on my piano skills. I've been learning this tricky classical piece lately—it's a challenge, but I love it."

Robin looked impressed. "I didn't know you were into music. That's awesome."

"Thanks," Alex said, smiling. "Maybe one day, I'll play something for the team. If we ever need a theme song, you know where to find me."

Tommy, their goalkeeper, joined in. "I've been working on something, too, but it's not music. I've been tinkering with this old RC car I found. I'm trying to modify it to go faster. It's not exactly soccer-related, but it's fun."

"You're a total nerd, Tommy," Dylan said, but his tone was affectionate.

"And proud of it," Tommy replied, grinning.

The conversation flowed easily, and Robin couldn't help but feel a sense of warmth. They weren't just a team—they were friends, each with their own quirks and interests. Moments like this reminded him why he loved being part of this group.

As dessert plates were being cleared away, Coach Thompson stood at the head of the table, raising his glass to get everyone's attention. The chatter quieted as all eyes turned to him.

"Alright, team," he began, a rare smile softening his usual stern expression. "First of all, I want to thank you all for being here tonight. It's moments like this that remind me why I love coaching."

The kids exchanged smiles, the mood in the room shifting to something more reflective.

"This dinner isn't just about celebrating the start of a new season," Coach continued. "It's about setting the tone for what's ahead. We've come a long way as a team, but there's always room to grow. And this season, as you all know, we're focusing on something that's not always glamorous—defending."

He paused, letting his words settle. "Defending is hard work. It takes discipline, focus, and a willingness to put the team above yourself. It's about protecting each other and making sure we're solid as a unit. Tackling, marking, intercepting—it's not just about stopping goals. It's about setting the foundation for everything else."

The kids nodded, their expressions serious. Robin felt a surge of pride, knowing that they were ready to rise to the challenge.

"But," Coach added, his tone lightening, "that doesn't mean we can't have fun along the way. Football isn't just about winning—it's about enjoying the game, growing as players, and building the kind of friendships that last a lifetime."

He raised his glass higher. "So here's to the season ahead. To hard work, to teamwork, and to defending with everything we've got."

The team raised their glasses—or, in the kids' case, their water and soda glasses—echoing Coach's toast. "To the season!"

As the dinner wound down, the team posed for a group photo, laughing and jostling for position. Ollie, of course, struck a dramatic pose, earning groans and laughter in equal measure.

Robin walked home with his parents, the cool evening air refreshing after the warmth of the restaurant. He thought about the night's conversations, Coach's speech, and the season ahead. They had a lot of work to do, but moments like this reminded him why it was all worth it.

This was more than a team—it was a family. And together, they could take on anything.

The Low Block

Defending deep isn't about retreating—it's about holding firm and standing tall.

The last ten minutes of the game felt like an eternity. The opposition, growing desperate to find a winner, pushed forward with everything they had. Their relentless attacks bore down on Robin's team, forcing every player to dig deeper than they ever had before.

"Stay tight, stay tight!" Tommy shouted, his voice hoarse from directing the defence all game. He stood on high alert, watching as the ball pinged back and forth just outside the penalty area.

The opposition's midfield orchestrated another attack, switching the ball swiftly from the left wing to the right, trying to stretch the Low Block. Dylan and Alex shuffled together, reading the movement and closing down the gaps.

"Mark your man!" Dylan bellowed, sweat dripping from his brow as he stayed glued to their towering striker, who had been causing problems all game.

Ollie, having tracked back to support the defence, lunged into a tackle, barely tipping the ball out for a corner. He got up quickly, his hands on his knees, panting.

"Good work, Ollie," Robin encouraged, though his voice betrayed the exhaustion they all felt.

The opposition lined up for the corner, their players crowding the box. Robin found himself marking their playmaker, a wiry and quick-footed player who had been instrumental in their attack all game.

The ball soared into the box, curling toward the far post. Their centre-back, a towering figure, rose above everyone else. For a moment, time seemed to freeze as his header thundered toward the goal.

Tommy, moving purely on instinct, flung himself to his left. His outstretched hand just managed to push the ball onto the post, where it ricocheted back into the chaos of the box.

"Clear it!" someone screamed.

Alex reacted first, sliding in to boot the ball away from danger. It flew out to the wing, but the opposition quickly regained possession, sending it back into the fray.

The ball bounced awkwardly in the penalty area, players from both teams lunging for it. Dylan threw himself in front of a shot, the ball smacking against his shin and spinning high into the air. Robin leapt to head it clear, but the opposition's playmaker anticipated it, chesting it down and setting himself up for a volley.

Robin's heart raced as the playmaker unleashed a thunderous shot. Dylan, still recovering from his earlier block, launched himself sideways, his body acting as a human shield. The ball struck his side and deflected wide.

The referee signalled for another corner, and Robin quickly jogged to his teammates, trying to rally them. "Come on, guys! Just a few more minutes. We've got this!"

Dylan, wincing as he straightened up, gave a nod. "Not letting them through," he said through gritted teeth.

The next corner was just as dangerous. The opposition tried a short pass to their winger, who whipped the ball in low and fast. Tommy shouted, "Leave it!" and dived onto the ball, clutching it tightly as players scrambled around him. He stayed on the ground for a moment, letting everyone reset, before leaping to his feet and launching the ball upfield.

Robin sprinted to collect the clearance, but the opposition midfielder beat him to it, sending the ball straight back toward their attackers. The pressure was unrelenting, and Robin could feel the strain in his legs as he chased down every pass, trying to intercept and break up their rhythm.

With two minutes left on the clock, the opposition earned a free kick just outside the box. The entire stadium seemed to hold its breath as their playmaker stepped up, eyeing the top corner.

Tommy crouched low, his eyes locked on the ball. The whistle blew, and the playmaker curled the shot over the wall. Robin watched in horror as the ball seemed destined for the net. But Tommy, in a moment of brilliance, leapt high and punched the ball over the crossbar.

The crowd erupted in cheers, and Tommy's teammates rushed to him, clapping him on the back. "You're a legend, Tommy!" Ollie shouted.

The referee signalled for three minutes of added time, and Robin's heart sank. They weren't out of the woods yet. The opposition continued to press, their desperation turning into frenzied attacks. Robin, Ollie, Dylan, and Alex worked tirelessly, throwing themselves into tackles, blocking shots, and clearing the ball whenever possible.

In the dying seconds, the opposition sent one final cross into the box. Their striker rose for the header, but Alex, leaping alongside him, managed to deflect it just enough to send it wide of the post. The referee's whistle blew, and the game ended in a 1-1 draw.

Robin collapsed onto the pitch, his chest heaving as he tried to catch his breath. Around him, his teammates did the same, exhaustion and relief etched on their faces.

As they walked off the field, Coach Thompson met them with a smile. "That," he said, his voice filled with pride, "was a team effort. We were under pressure the entire second half, but you stayed disciplined and showed heart. That's how we hold the line."

Robin, still catching his breath, looked at his teammates and smiled. They had struggled, they had been tested, but they had held firm. It wasn't the win they had hoped for, but it felt like a victory nonetheless.

Dylan nudged Robin as they headed to the locker room. "We survived that, mate. Next time, we'll do more than survive."

Robin grinned. "Next time, we'll win."

Transition Defence - Building from Reflection

When the whistle blows, it's not just skill that matters—it's the will to endure.

The sun hung high over the training ground as Robin jogged onto the pitch. The memory of their 1-1 draw still weighed on his mind. The final minutes of the game had been intense, a whirlwind of frantic defending and scrambling for the ball. He could see the same reflection in the faces of his teammates as they gathered in a circle near Coach Thompson. Today's session was going to be about learning from that chaos.

Coach Thompson stood in the centre of the group, clipboard in hand, his tone firm but encouraging. "Alright, team," he began, looking each player in the eye, "let's talk about the weekend's game. It was a battle, and you held on, but those last ten minutes? We made it a lot harder on ourselves than we needed to. Let's break down why."

Robin exchanged glances with Dylan and Ollie. They all knew exactly what Coach meant. The team had dropped too deep, leaving massive gaps in midfield. The opposition had exploited those spaces relentlessly, pushing them to their limits.

Coach gestured to a whiteboard he had set up on the sideline, marked with a rough diagram of their formation during those final moments. "What do you see here?" he asked, pointing at the defensive line crammed just outside their penalty box.

"We were pinned back," Dylan said, stepping forward. "We weren't closing down the spaces in front of us, so they kept driving into the gaps."

"Exactly," Coach replied. "And when we did win the ball back, what happened?"

"We panicked," Ollie admitted, kicking at the grass. "We just booted it away instead of looking for an option."

Coach nodded, his expression softening. "That's right. And that's what we're going to fix today. Transition defence isn't just about running back—it's about reacting as a unit, closing the gaps, and turning defence into attack when the opportunity comes. Let's get started."

As the players dispersed to begin warm-ups, Robin couldn't help but feel a surge of determination. The drills today weren't just about technique; they were about learning to stay calm under pressure.

The first drill started with a compact recovery exercise. Coach split the team into two groups—attackers and defenders. Robin found himself paired with Alex and Dylan, working on their ability to regain their shape quickly after losing possession. As soon as the attackers took the ball, Coach blew his whistle, and Robin sprang into action, sprinting to close down the ball carrier.

"Good, Robin!" Coach shouted. "Now, where's the support?"

Alex and Dylan immediately dropped back into position, cutting off passing lanes and forcing the attackers wide. Robin could feel the difference already; it wasn't about chasing blindly after the ball but about working together to stay organised.

"Perfect!" Coach clapped as the defenders regained possession. "See how much easier it is when you move as a unit?"

As they reset, Robin turned to Alex with a grin. "That actually felt controlled. We weren't just running around like headless chickens this time."

"Speak for yourself," Alex teased, brushing sweat from his forehead. "I still feel like I'm chasing shadows."

The session moved on to pressure and cover drills. Coach had set up a grid with marked zones, challenging the defenders to press the ball carrier while covering for each other. Robin worked with Dylan and Tommy, who had come out of goal to participate in the outfield drills.

As the attackers pushed into their zone, Robin moved in to press the ball, his timing sharp. Dylan shifted behind him, ready to cover if the attacker tried to pass. Robin managed to force a rushed pass, which Tommy intercepted cleanly.

"That's the way!" Coach called from the sideline. "Robin, great pressure. Dylan, excellent cover. Tommy, sharp reading of the play."

During a water break, Robin turned to Tommy with a grin. "You might be too good at this, Tommy. You're making the rest of us look bad."

Tommy laughed, shrugging. "Hey, I've got to make sure you keep me from getting battered in the goal. Call it self-preservation."

The banter lightened the mood, but Robin could see how focused everyone was. They weren't just training— they were learning to trust each other.

Coach then introduced a drill focused on turning defence into attack. This time, Robin's team was tasked with winning the ball and transitioning quickly into a counterattack. The key was composure: no rushed clearances, no panicked passes. Just quick, calculated movements to move the ball forward.

Robin found himself in the thick of it when Ollie won the ball back in midfield. "Robin, left!" Ollie shouted, sending a crisp pass his way. Robin turned, spotting Jake making a run down the flank. Without hesitation, he played the ball into Jake's path, who whipped a cross into the box.

Even though the move didn't result in a goal, Coach was ecstatic. "That's how you do it!" he yelled. "Win it back, move it forward, and create options. Keep building on that."

By the end of the session, the players were exhausted but buzzing with energy. They could feel the progress they had made and the difference it would make in the next game. As they gathered around Coach for a final talk, he looked at them with pride.

"You're getting there," he said. "Transition defence isn't just about running–it's about thinking. And today, you showed me you can do both. Next week, we'll take this a step further with some positional drills. But for now, great work."

As they walked off the pitch, Robin felt lighter. The reflection from their last game wasn't a burden anymore– it was a lesson. And he couldn't wait to put what they'd learned into practice.

A Game of Two Halves

The best defence is one that transitions with clarity and finishes with purpose.

The sun beat down on the field as Robin stood in the centre circle, the ball at his feet, waiting for the referee to blow the whistle. Today's match wasn't just another friendly—it was their first real test since the start of the season. Their opponents were known for their swift counterattacks and disciplined defence. Robin felt a twinge of nervousness but pushed it aside, glancing around at his teammates, each of them focused and ready.

Ollie gave him a quick thumbs-up from the wing, Jake stretched his legs in midfield, and Tommy adjusted his gloves in goal. The referee raised his hand, and with a sharp whistle, the game began.

The whistle blew, and Robin's team immediately took control of the ball. The energy on the field was electric, with the team pushing forward with purpose. Robin, now accustomed to leading the play, orchestrated their attacks with precision, sending the ball wide to Ollie on the left wing and linking up with Jake in midfield. Their confidence was evident, but the opposition was quick, disciplined, and waiting for a moment to pounce.

Fifteen minutes into the game, Robin received the ball in midfield and spotted Alex making a darting run down the right. With a sharp pass, Robin threaded the ball between two defenders, and Alex sprinted to meet it. He controlled the ball skillfully and drove toward the edge of the box. The crowd buzzed in anticipation as Alex attempted a clever one-two with Ollie, but a defender intercepted the return pass.

The interception triggered an immediate counterattack. The opposition's winger, a blur of speed, picked up the loose ball and surged forward. Dylan, playing as a central defender, sprinted to close him down but couldn't keep pace. Robin turned on his heels and rushed back, yelling, "Track back! Cover the space!"

The winger sent a perfectly weighted cross into the box, and the opposition's striker was already in position. Dylan dived in to block the shot but missed, and the striker slammed the ball into the bottom corner.

0-1.

Dylan clenched his fists, visibly frustrated. Robin jogged over, patting him on the back. "Don't worry, we'll get it back," Robin said, though he felt the sting of the goal himself. The team regrouped, determined not to let the setback define them.

The goal seemed to shake them, but it also lit a fire in their bellies. For the next ten minutes, the team tightened up their play. Coach Thompson's voice rang from the sideline, "Stay compact! Don't lose your shape!"

Robin dropped deeper into midfield, focusing on keeping possession. After a patient build-up, Jake attempted a lofted ball over the defence, aiming for Ollie. But once again, the opposition intercepted, and this time, their midfield surged forward as a unit, quickly outnumbering Robin's team in transition.

"Get back!" Robin shouted as he sprinted after the ball. Jake was the first to react, chasing down the opposition's attacking midfielder. The player tried to cut inside, but Jake stuck out a foot, nicking the ball away. Dylan and Alex, now in position, cleared the danger with a firm pass back to Tommy, who took his time to reset the play.

The team breathed a collective sigh of relief. Jake clapped his hands and shouted, "Come on, boys! Stay sharp!" Robin jogged over to fist-bump him. "Great work, Jake," he said, feeling the team's confidence start to rebuild.

With halftime approaching, Robin's team pushed forward again. They were desperate to equalise, and the pressure they applied forced the opposition into a few mistakes. Alex took a shot from a distance that skimmed just over the bar, and Ollie's cross into the box nearly found Robin, but the goalkeeper punched it away at the last second.

The intensity of their attacks, however, left gaps in their shape. In the 40th minute, the opposition capitalised on one such gap. Jake, pressing high, lost the ball to a sharp tackle. The opposition midfielder quickly sent a long ball over the top, bypassing the midfield entirely.

Dylan, under pressure, hesitated for a split second, unsure whether to commit to the ball or drop back. That moment of hesitation was all the striker needed. He slipped past Dylan and met the ball with a controlled touch. Tommy rushed off his line, but the striker calmly slotted the ball past him.

0-2.

Dylan dropped his head, hands on his hips. "That's on me," he muttered as Tommy jogged over to offer encouragement. Robin could see the frustration building in the team, but he knew they couldn't afford to let it spiral.

"Shake it off!" Robin shouted, clapping his hands. "We've still got another half. Let's keep it together."

The halftime whistle blew, and the team trudged off the pitch. The scoreline was harsh, but Robin knew they had shown glimpses of their potential. They just needed to stay disciplined and respond in the second half. As they gathered around Coach Thompson, the tension was palpable.

Coach took a deep breath before addressing them. "We've been caught out twice, but this isn't the end. You've shown that you can track back and defend as a unit. Now, it's about doing it every time, not just most of the time. Stay organised, stay smart, and let's turn this around."

Robin nodded, exchanging determined looks with Ollie and Jake. The first half had been a lesson, and now it was time to show they could learn from it.

The team returned to the pitch with renewed determination. Coach Thompson's halftime talk had refocused their minds. While they were still down 2-0, Robin could see the fire in his teammates' eyes. They knew they couldn't afford to let the opposition control the game any longer. This was their chance to prove they had learned from their mistakes.

The opposition wasted no time testing Robin's team in the second half. Within five minutes, they launched another attack, this time down the left wing. Their winger danced past Alex, who had been caught slightly out of position. The crowd roared as the opposition surged toward the penalty area.

Robin sprinted back, calling to Dylan and Jake, "Hold the line! Cover the middle!" The winger delivered a low cross into the box, aiming for their striker. Dylan, now fully locked in, read the play perfectly. He stepped in front of the striker, timing his interception flawlessly. With a calm pass, he sent the ball to Jake, who cleared it upfield.

"That's how you do it!" Jake shouted, clapping Dylan on the back as they jogged up the field to reset.

Tommy, who had watched the sequence from the goal, yelled, "Great work, lads! Let's keep it tight!"

The successful defence brought a surge of confidence to the team. Robin could feel their energy shifting. They were no longer scrambling to contain the opposition—they were defending with intent and intelligence.

With the score still 2-0, Robin's team began to push forward, eager to get on the scoreboard. Ollie, full of energy, made a blistering run down the left flank. Robin spotted him and sent a precise pass through two defenders, landing perfectly at Ollie's feet. Ollie cut inside and took a shot, but the ball struck a defender and bounced away.

The opposition seized the moment to counterattack. Their midfield quickly transitioned, sending the ball to their forward, who raced past the halfway line. Robin immediately turned back, shouting, "Get back! Track him!"

This time, the team reacted as one. Alex closed in from the left, forcing the forward to slow down. Jake darted back to cut off the passing lane while Dylan stayed central, anticipating the striker's movement. Robin positioned himself just outside the box, ready to intercept.

The forward hesitated, and in that brief moment, Jake lunged forward, cleanly winning the ball. He turned and passed it to Robin, who wasted no time launching a counter of their own. The opposition had been caught off guard by the swift transition.

Robin saw Ollie making a run down the left again and played a long, curling pass. Ollie took it in stride and sent a cross into the box. This time, their striker was ready. He leapt into the air and smashed the ball into the net with a powerful header.

1-2.

The team erupted in celebration, their first goal reigniting their hope. Robin ran over to Jake, grinning. "That tackle was perfect, mate. Just what we needed."

Jake smiled back, a look of satisfaction on his face. "We're not done yet."

The final ten minutes of the game were tense. The opposition, clearly shaken by the goal, pushed forward again. Robin's team held their shape, defending as a unit. Tommy made a crucial save, diving low to stop a fierce shot from the edge of the box. The clock ticked on, but Robin could sense an opportunity brewing.

With five minutes left, the team found themselves in possession. Robin picked up the ball near the centre circle and drove forward, scanning the field. Jake was making a run into space while Ollie hovered on the wing, waiting for his chance.

Robin faked a pass to Ollie, drawing two defenders toward him, then slipped the ball to Jake. Jake controlled it with one touch and sent a quick pass to Alex, who had darted into the box. Alex took a shot, but the goalkeeper parried it, sending the ball bouncing back into the middle of the penalty area.

Robin, having continued his run, found himself in the perfect position. Without hesitating, he struck the ball low and hard. It flew past the goalkeeper and into the net.

2-2.

The crowd erupted as Robin's teammates rushed to him, their faces lit with joy. "That's how it's done!" Ollie shouted, throwing an arm around Robin's shoulder.

"You didn't give up," Dylan said, patting Robin on the back. "None of us did."

The final minutes of the game were a battle of endurance. The opposition, desperate to reclaim the lead, threw everything they had at Robin's team. Dylan and Alex were relentless in defence, clearing cross after cross. Tommy made one final save in the dying seconds, leaping to tip a long-range shot over the bar.

The referee blew the whistle, and the game ended in a hard-fought 2-2 draw.

As they gathered on the pitch after the game, Coach Thompson approached the team, a satisfied smile on his face. "That," he said, "is what I call progress. You didn't panic; you adjusted, and you fought back. We're not perfect yet, but today, you showed what it means to play as a team."

Robin looked around at his teammates, their faces tired but proud. They had faced challenges and made mistakes, but they had also shown resilience and teamwork.

As they walked off the pitch together, Robin felt a sense of accomplishment. The season was far from over, but this game had proven that they were growing stronger with every challenge they faced.

Defensive Mastery in 4-4-2

Every position has its role; every role has its responsibility—master both, and you master the game.

The cool autumn breeze swept across the training ground as Robin stepped onto the pitch with his teammates. It was their second week of training since the season began, and there was a new buzz of energy in the air. Coach Thompson had promised to focus on tactical formations this week, and as the team huddled together, Robin noticed an intensity in the coach's expression.

"Alright, listen up," Coach Thompson began, his hands on his hips. "Today, we're diving into one of the most tried-and-tested formations in soccer: the 4-4-2. It's simple, effective, and, when done right, incredibly tough to break down."

Robin exchanged a quick glance with Jake, who was standing beside him. Jake, ever the tactical thinker, already seemed intrigued, nodding slightly at the coach's words.

Coach walked toward the whiteboard that he had set up on the sidelines, where a basic diagram of the 4-4-2 was drawn. "The 4-4-2 is built around two strong lines of defence," he explained, tapping the board. "The back four and the midfield four work together to keep the opposition out while the two forwards apply pressure up top. It's about discipline, communication, and keeping your shape."

Robin listened intently, his mind racing. He had seen teams use this formation on TV but had never thought about the intricacies involved. Coach's voice cut through his thoughts.

"In this system, the key is compactness," Coach continued. "The defensive and midfield lines need to stay close together to prevent gaps. If one of you is out of position, it opens space for the opposition to exploit. That means constant communication and movement as a unit."

Jake raised his hand, his curiosity getting the better of him. "Coach, what happens if the wingers push too far forward? Doesn't that leave the full-backs exposed?"

"Good question, Jake," Coach said, smiling. "That's where balance comes in. The wide midfielders—Ollie and Robin—need to know when to push up and when to drop back. It's about reading the game and supporting your teammates. We'll get into that during the drills."

The team spread out across the pitch as Coach began setting up the first drill. Cones were arranged in a grid to divide the field into zones, with markers for defenders, midfielders, and forwards. Robin took his place on the left side of midfield, glancing at Ollie, who was on the right. Jake and Dylan lined up as the central defensive pair, with Tommy directing them from his goal.

"Alright," Coach called out, pacing along the sideline. "This drill is about understanding your zones. As I move the ball around, you need to adjust your positions. Stay compact, keep your shape, and communicate. Remember, this isn't about chasing the ball—it's about controlling space."

As Coach passed the ball between mannequins representing the opposition, the team shifted together, following the movement of the ball. Robin focused on maintaining the line with Jake and Dylan, listening for their shouts to step forward or drop back.

"Shift left!" Jake called as the ball moved toward the wing. Robin quickly adjusted his position, ensuring there was no gap between him and the central midfielder. Ollie, on the opposite side, mirrored his movements, keeping the midfield balanced.

Coach blew the whistle, stopping the drill. "Good! Now, remember, when the ball moves quickly, you need to react even faster. Let's run it again, but this time, I want to see sharper communication."

As they repeated the drill, Robin began to feel more confident in his role. The constant shouts from Jake and Tommy helped him stay in position, and he noticed how the formation started to feel like a solid wall, hard for the imaginary opposition to penetrate.

The next drill focused on transitioning from attack to defence. Coach split the team into two groups, with one attacking and the other defending in the 4-4-2 shape. Robin's group started on defence, while the attackers, led by Alex and Mason, aimed to exploit any gaps in their formation.

"When you lose the ball," Coach explained, "you need to drop back into your defensive shape immediately. The key is to recover quickly and prevent the opposition from taking advantage of your transition."

As the drill began, Robin watched as Alex received the ball on the wing and charged forward. Ollie sprinted back to cover, forcing Alex to pass inside to Mason. Robin quickly closed down Mason, cutting off his options and forcing him to play backwards. The team held their shape, and the attackers struggled to find a way through.

"That's it!" Coach shouted. "Stay compact, force them wide, and don't let them play through the middle."

On the next play, the defenders lost their shape as Alex played a quick one-two with Mason. Jake stepped out of position to challenge, leaving a gap in the backline. Mason slipped a pass through to Dylan, who was playing as a makeshift striker for the drill. Dylan fired a shot past Tommy, who shook his head in frustration.

"See what happens when we lose our shape?" Coach said, gesturing at the team. "One mistake, and it opens everything up. Let's run it again, and this time, stay disciplined."

Despite the intense focus, there were light-hearted moments that kept the team motivated. When Robin accidentally tripped while trying to block Alex, the others burst into laughter.

"Careful, Robin," Jake teased. "We're defending, not auditioning for a diving competition!"

"Yeah, yeah," Robin replied, grinning as he picked himself up. "At least I'm putting in the effort!"

Even Coach joined in the laughter, though he quickly got them back on track. "Alright, enough jokes. Let's focus. Robin, next time, stay on your feet."

For the third drill, Coach Thompson set up a scenario designed to help the team transition from defence to attack while staying organised. He divided the players into two groups again, with one defending in the 4-4-2 and the other attacking. The focus was on intercepting the ball and launching a quick counterattack.

"Alright, listen up," Coach called out. "In a real game, when you win the ball back, you need to transition quickly into attack. The 4-4-2 gives us a solid defensive shape, but it's also great for counterattacking. Robin, Ollie, and Jake, you'll be key in this drill. When we regain possession, I want you to think two moves ahead—where's the space? Who's making the run? And how can you break their defence open?"

The drill began with the attacking team trying to break down the defenders. Alex, playing as the opposition's playmaker, sent a looping ball over the defence toward Mason, who was sprinting into the box. Dylan, positioned as a central defender, anticipated the pass and intercepted it with a well-timed header.

"Good, Dylan!" Coach shouted. "Now counter!"

Dylan immediately passed the ball to Jake, who was stationed in the central midfield. Jake looked up and spotted Ollie making a run down the right flank. With a sharp pass, Jake sent the ball wide. Ollie controlled it, sprinted toward the opposition's box, and crossed it into the middle, where Robin was waiting.

Robin met the ball with a first-time shot, but it went just over the bar. "Unlucky, Robin!" Coach encouraged. "That was the right idea. Let's try it again."

As the drill progressed, the team began to find their rhythm. On one play, they executed a perfect counterattack. Dylan intercepted a through ball and passed it to Jake, who found Ollie. This time, Robin's shot was on target, forcing a diving save from Tommy, who was playing as the opposition's goalkeeper.

"That's it!" Coach said, clapping his hands. "Quick, decisive, and coordinated. That's how we counter from the 4-4-2."

To wrap up the session, Coach Thompson introduced a final drill designed to simulate a high-pressure scenario. The defending team was tasked with maintaining their 4-4-2 shape while the attacking team pressed relentlessly.

"Here's the challenge," Coach explained. "The attacking team will have five minutes to score. Defenders, your job is to stay disciplined, communicate, and clear the ball when needed. If you can hold them off for the full five minutes, you win."

The drill began, and the attackers wasted no time piling on the pressure. Alex and Mason combined well in midfield, sending wave after wave of attacks toward the defenders. Dylan and Jake were vocal, shouting instructions to Robin and Ollie to drop back and help cover the wings.

"Shift left! Tighten up!" Jake yelled as Alex played a pass out wide. Robin sprinted back to block the cross, deflecting it out for a corner.

As the minutes ticked by, the defenders held their ground. In one play, Mason finds a gap and unleashes a powerful shot, but Tommy is there to make a spectacular save, diving low to his left.

"Great save, Tommy!" Ollie cheered, clapping his hands. The defenders rallied around their goalkeeper, determined to see out the drill.

In the final seconds, Alex tried one last attempt, sending a lofted ball into the box. Dylan rose high to clear it with a header, and as the whistle blew, the defenders erupted in cheers.

"Well done, everyone," Coach said, smiling. "That's the kind of discipline and teamwork we need in real games. Remember, the 4-4-2 isn't just about defending—it's about defending as a team."

As the team gathered around Coach for the final talk, the atmosphere was a mix of exhaustion and pride. They had worked hard, and it showed.

"You all did great today," Coach said, his tone encouraging. "The 4-4-2 is a classic formation for a reason—it works. But only if everyone knows their role and works together. Keep practising, and this will become second nature."

Robin glanced at his teammates, their tired faces lit up with smiles. It had been a challenging session, but they had learned a lot. As they packed up and prepared to head home, Robin felt a sense of accomplishment. The 4-4-2 was beginning to make sense, and he knew it would be a key part of their strategy for the season.

As they walked off the pitch, Jake turned to Robin. "So, what do you think about the 4-4-2? Feels like we're building a wall out there."

Robin grinned. "Yeah, a wall that can counterattack like lightning. I think we're onto something."

The team laughed, their spirits high as they headed into the rest of their week, ready to put their newfound knowledge into action.

The Test of the 4-4-2

Big challenges aren't meant to crush us; they're meant to show how far we've come.

The sun was shining brightly as Robin and his teammates arrived at the pitch for their next game. This time, the stakes felt higher. It wasn't just another friendly or a scrimmage; they were about to test the defensive formation they had been practising all week. The 4-4-2 system, as Coach Thompson had explained, was about balance—defensive solidity and sharp counterattacks. Today would be the true test of whether they had mastered it.

Robin, standing with Jake and Dylan on the sideline, adjusted his shin pads and glanced at the opposition warming up. They looked sharp, fast, and composed. It was clear this game would be no walk in the park.

"Alright, team!" Coach Thompson called out, gathering the players into a huddle. His expression was calm but serious. "Today's game is about execution. We've been working hard on the 4-4-2, and now it's time to put it into practice. Stay disciplined, communicate, and trust each other. This formation works when every single one of you does your part."

Robin nodded, feeling a mix of anticipation and nerves. Jake gave him a reassuring pat on the back. "We've got this, mate. Just remember your runs."

Dylan, standing on Robin's other side, grinned. "And don't forget to put one in the net for us."

Robin laughed, the tension easing slightly. As the referee's whistle blew, the team took their positions, ready for the battle ahead.

The game started evenly, with both teams feeling each other out. Robin's team stuck closely to their formation, maintaining their lines and focusing on their shape. The first opportunity fell to Robin after Jake intercepted a pass in midfield and played the ball out wide to Ollie.

"Robin, make the run!" Ollie shouted, already sprinting down the wing.

Robin darted toward the box, weaving between defenders as Ollie crossed the ball in. Timing his run perfectly, Robin connected with a header that flew straight at the goalkeeper, who caught it cleanly.

"Unlucky, Robin!" Jake called out from midfield. "Keep going. The next one's yours."

Though the chance didn't result in a goal, it showed their potential to threaten on the counterattack.

As the game progressed, the opposition began to find their rhythm. Their midfielders moved the ball quickly, probing for gaps in the 4-4-2 setup. Twenty minutes in, their left winger burst down the sideline, outpacing Dylan.

"Dylan, track back!" Tommy shouted from goal, but the winger was already cutting inside.

The cross came in hard and low, zipping past Jake and Alex in the centre. Tommy lunged for it but fumbled the clearance. The ball fell to the feet of the opposition striker, who tapped it into the net.

"Come on, guys! We need to talk more!" Jake yelled, clapping his hands to rally the team. Dylan jogged back, his frustration evident.

"Sorry, that's on me," Dylan muttered, shaking his head.

Robin jogged over and gave him a reassuring nudge. "Don't sweat it, Dylan. We'll get it back."

The team didn't let the goal demoralise them. Jake took charge in midfield, barking instructions and encouraging everyone to stay focused. Ten minutes later, their perseverance paid off.

Jake intercepted a sloppy pass in midfield, immediately looking up to spot Ollie darting down the wing. With a perfectly weighted ball, Jake sent Ollie sprinting into space.

"Robin, back post!" Ollie called as he whipped in a cross.

Robin sprinted into the box, leapt high, and powered a header past the goalkeeper. The net rippled, and the team erupted in celebration.

"Great ball, Ollie!" Robin shouted, grinning as his teammates crowded around him.

"That was all you, mate," Ollie replied, ruffling Robin's hair.

The equaliser energised the team, and for a brief moment, they had the momentum.

Just before half-time, the opposition struck again. A miscommunication between Alex and Jake in midfield led to a costly turnover. Their attacking midfielder seized the loose ball and threaded a pass to the striker, who broke through the defensive line.

"Track him, Dylan!" Tommy yelled, but it was too late. The striker rounded the keeper and slotted the ball into an empty net.

Robin clenched his fists in frustration as the whistle blew for half-time. They were down 2-1, and the mood in the locker room was sombre.

In the locker room, Coach Thompson addressed the team. "Listen, we've shown we can play in this formation, but we're making it too easy for them to exploit mistakes. Communication and composure—those are the keys. We're still in this game, but we need to step it up in the second half."

Robin nodded along with his teammates, determined to turn things around. "Let's go out there and give it everything," he said, earning murmurs of agreement from the group.

The opposition came out strong in the second half, determined to extend their lead. For the first ten minutes, Robin's team was pinned back, defending wave after wave of attacks. Tommy made a crucial save, tipping a long-range shot over the bar.

On the resulting corner, Dylan redeemed himself by rising above the opposition striker and clearing the ball with a powerful header.

"Brilliant, Dylan!" Jake shouted as the team regained their shape.

Midway through the half, Robin's team found their rhythm again. After winning the ball in midfield, Jake played it to Ollie, who danced past two defenders. Robin made a run toward the near post, but Ollie spotted Alex arriving late on the edge of the box.

"Alex, it's yours!" Ollie shouted, cutting the ball back.

Alex struck it first-time, sending the ball sailing into the top corner. The crowd erupted as the scoreline read 2-2.

Despite a frantic final ten minutes, neither team managed to score again. The match ended in a 2-2 draw, and though they hadn't won, Robin's team felt proud of their performance.

As they gathered on the sideline, Coach Thompson smiled. "This was a tough game, but you showed resilience. We'll work on the mistakes, but for now, be proud of how you fought."

Robin exchanged high-fives with his teammates, already looking forward to the next challenge. This was only the beginning of their journey with the 4-4-2 formation.

Defensive Strength in 4-2-3-1

In defence, strength comes not from a single player but from the collective trust of the team.

The air was heavy with determination as the team gathered for their weekly training session. The previous game, a challenging loss in the 4-4-2 formation, still lingered in their minds. They had fought hard, but the defeat highlighted glaring gaps in their defensive approach, leaving the players eager to improve. The sun peeked through the clouds as Coach Thompson strolled onto the pitch, a clipboard in hand and a thoughtful expression on his face.

"All right, everyone, bring it in," Coach called, his voice steady but firm. The players jogged over, forming a semi-circle around him. Robin glanced around at his teammates, noticing the mix of anticipation and focus etched on their faces. Dylan was nervously adjusting his shin pads, Jake looked deep in thought, and Alex twirled a blade of grass between his fingers.

"Before we jump into today's session, let's reflect on the last game," Coach began. "It was a tough one, no doubt about that. We struggled with transitions and left gaps in our defence. But here's the thing—every challenge is a lesson, and every lesson is an opportunity to grow."

The players nodded silently, some glancing at each other as Coach continued. "Jake, you were vocal, which was good, but sometimes a bit too reactive. You need to give constructive instructions, not just shout. Dylan, your last-ditch clearance was excellent, but you can't rely on heroics every time. Positioning needs to be your first line of defence."

Dylan scratched the back of his head, giving a sheepish grin. "Got it, Coach. No more last-minute drama."

The group chuckled, and Coach smiled. "Robin, your runs were great, but as a playmaker, you need to think one step ahead. Remember, defence starts from the front. And Alex, your equaliser was brilliant, but I want you to work on tracking back more. Everyone on this team contributes to defence."

Alex gave a thumbs-up, his grin as wide as the pitch. "Noted, Coach."

With the feedback delivered, Coach turned serious. "Today, we're shifting gears. We're moving into the 4-2-3-1 formation. It's more defensively solid and will help us control the game better. But to make it work, we need discipline, communication, and, above all, trust in each other."

The coach brought out the tactical board and placed markers to represent the formation. "In this setup, the two holding midfielders act as our defensive shield. They'll disrupt attacks, cover gaps, and link the defence to the attack. The back four stays compact, while the advanced midfielders provide width and creativity. It's all about balance."

He moved the markers to show how the team should shift when defending. "When the opposition attacks down the flanks, the holding midfielders shift to cover the space while the backline remains tight. The advanced midfielders track back to help, creating layers of defence. And when we win the ball back, we transition quickly, using our width to exploit gaps."

Robin leaned in, absorbing every detail. He could already see how the new formation would help them stay more compact and organised.

The first drill of the day focused on the two defensive midfielders, with Jake and Alex taking on the roles. They stood in front of the backline as Coach explained their task. "Your job is to anticipate passes, cut off channels, and shield the defence. Work as a unit—if one presses, the other holds. Communication is key."

The attackers—led by Robin and Ollie—tested their resolve. Robin darted forward, looking for gaps, but Jake stepped in, intercepting a pass and quickly laying it off to Alex, who launched a counterattack. "Good work!" Coach called. "That's how you control the space."

Ollie smirked. "Next time, Jake, I'm slipping past you."

Jake grinned. "Keep dreaming, mate."

In the next drill, the entire defensive unit practised shifting as a block. Coach had set up cones to simulate the opposition's movement. "Stay compact, keep your lines tight, and don't let the ball carrier have time to think," he instructed.

The players moved as a cohesive unit, adjusting their positions based on the ball's location. When Robin received the ball, Dylan stepped up to press, forcing him to pass back. The other defenders quickly shifted to cover the space, denying Robin any chance to exploit gaps.

Coach nodded approvingly. "That's what I want to see—pressure without losing shape. Well done."

The final drill simulated real-game scenarios where the team lost possession while attacking. "When we lose the ball, we drop back into our shape immediately," Coach explained. "The quicker we recover, the harder it is for the opposition to counter."

Robin led the attack, combining with Ollie to create a chance. But when the defenders intercepted the ball, Jake and Alex sprinted back into position, cutting off the counterattack. Robin, not one to give up easily, pressed high, forcing the defender to clear the ball under pressure.

Dylan clapped his hands. "That's how we do it—team defence!"

As the sun dipped lower in the sky, Coach gathered the team for a final talk. "You've all done well today. The 4-2-3-1 formation requires patience and discipline, but if we stick to it, we'll become a formidable defensive unit.

Remember, defence is not just about stopping goals—it's about controlling the game."

The players nodded their faces a mix of exhaustion and determination. Robin felt a surge of confidence. The new formation was challenging, but he could see how it would make them stronger. As they packed up their gear, Jake turned to Robin.

"Think we've got this 4-2-3-1 figured out?" he asked.

Robin smiled. "We're getting there. It's all about trusting the process."

With that, the team left the pitch, ready to put their newfound defensive strength to the test in the next game.

Facing the Local Rivals

Rivalries bring out the best and the worst, but they always teach us the most.

The morning sun gleamed down on the pitch as Robin and his teammates walked toward their familiar home ground. There was an unmistakable buzz in the air, one that could only mean one thing—it was derby day. The rivalry between their team and the neighbouring side had been alive for years, and the players felt the weight of history on their shoulders.

As they gathered near the benches, Robin looked around at his teammates. Alex was tying his boots with a look of determination, Ollie was juggling a ball to calm his nerves, and Dylan was already stretching, focused and serious.

Coach Thompson arrived, clipboard in hand, his expression a mix of calm and authority. "Alright, listen up," he started, addressing the group. "This isn't just any game. You know what this means. But don't let the occasion overwhelm you. Remember everything we've been working on—discipline, organisation, and teamwork. If we stick to the plan, we'll come out on top."

The team nodded, their confidence bolstered by the coach's words. Coach Thompson went on to review the tactics, emphasising the importance of maintaining their 4-2-3-1 defensive shape. "Stay compact in defence, but don't be afraid to press when the opportunity is there. And, Robin," he said, turning to him, "I want you to drop deep when needed. Be the link between defence and attack."

Robin gave a firm nod. He knew the role well by now and was ready to lead the charge.

The whistle blew, and the game kicked off. Right from the start, the rivals came out swinging, pressing high and looking to unsettle Robin's team. The ball moved quickly, and the pace of the game was relentless.

Fifteen minutes in, the rivals launched their first dangerous attack. Their playmaker found space in midfield and slipped a pass through to their striker. Dylan sprinted to close the gap, timing his sliding tackle perfectly and knocking the ball out of play just before the striker could shoot.

"Great tackle, Dylan!" shouted Tommy, their goalkeeper, clapping his gloves.

Robin jogged over to pat Dylan on the back. "That was close. Keep it up, yeah?"

Dylan nodded, his eyes fixed on the opposition, ready for the next wave.

The rivals' pressure didn't let up. Their midfielders moved the ball with speed, probing for gaps in the defence. Jake, playing as a defensive midfielder, tried to intercept a pass, but the ball slipped just beyond his reach.

The rival striker took advantage of the opening, darting into the box and firing a low shot past Tommy into the bottom corner.

"Come on, guys, heads up!" Robin shouted, clapping his hands to rally the team as the opposition celebrated. The score was now 1-0, but there was still plenty of time to fight back.

Determined to stay in the game, Robin's team tightened their defensive shape. The midfielders dropped back to support the defenders, and the full-backs stayed compact.

The rivals tried to exploit the wings, sending their winger darting down the left flank. Alex tracked back furiously, staying close to his man. As the winger sent in a cross, Alex stretched out his leg, deflecting the ball away and out for a throw-in.

"Nice one, Alex!" Ollie called out as he ran to reset.

Robin jogged over to Alex and gave him a thumbs-up. "Good recovery. Let's keep it tight."

The first half ended with the rivals leading 1-0. The team trudged off the pitch, frustrated but not defeated. In the changing room, Coach Thompson wasted no time addressing the group.

"Alright, we're only down by one," he said, his voice steady. "They've been strong, but we've had our moments. What's missing is confidence in the transition. Robin, I need you to take charge in the middle. Everyone else, remember, defending is a team effort. When we lose the ball, we track back as one."

Alex, still catching his breath, looked visibly nervous. "I'll try to stay tighter on my man, Coach."

"You're doing fine, Alex," Coach reassured him. "Just keep your head up and stay disciplined."

Robin glanced at Ollie. "We've got this. We just need to take our chances when they come."

Ollie grinned. "Yeah, and maybe we'll actually score this time."

The team chuckled, breaking the tension slightly. They walked back onto the pitch with renewed focus, ready for the second half.

The second half began with a burst of energy from Robin's team. Coach had instructed them to press higher up the pitch, and they executed it perfectly.

Robin led the charge, pressing the rival playmaker and forcing a loose pass. Jake intercepted it, quickly switching the ball out wide to Ollie. The winger sprinted down the line and whipped in a cross, but the rival goalkeeper punched it clear.

"Unlucky!" Tommy shouted from the back. "Keep it coming, lads!"

The team's pressing rattled the rivals, and they began to make mistakes.

The breakthrough finally came in the 60th minute. Robin, now dropping deeper to collect the ball, found Alex with a quick pass. Alex drove forward, passing to Ollie, who was waiting on the flank. With a deft touch, Ollie sent a curling cross into the box.

Robin timed his run perfectly, leaping above the defenders and heading the ball into the top corner. The crowd erupted in cheers as the scoreline read 1-1.

The game had reached a boiling point, with both teams pushing harder and the tension thick in the air. Every tackle, every pass, and every movement felt sharper, more urgent. The crowd's cheers and shouts echoed like a heartbeat through the stadium, urging the players forward. Robin's team had been holding their own, but the pressure was relentless.

Alex had been running tirelessly, tracking back and forth along the left flank. His breathing was heavy, sweat dripping from his brow as he tried to keep pace with the rival winger, who was quick, nimble, and relentless in his attacks. Each time the ball came near Alex's side, the winger seemed to find a way to slip past, forcing Alex to dig deeper into his reserves of energy and focus.

Then it happened. A long ball from the opposition's midfield arced high into the air, dropping perfectly at the winger's feet. Alex sprinted to close the gap, his heart pounding, adrenaline coursing through his veins. He could feel the urgency—the team was stretched, and if the winger broke free, it would leave their defence vulnerable.

The winger feinted left, then darted right, his quick footwork leaving Alex a half-step behind. Panic bubbled in Alex's chest as he saw the player racing toward the edge of the box. Desperation took over. Without thinking, Alex launched himself into a sliding tackle, his legs scything through the grass.

The contact was immediate and brutal. Alex's foot missed the ball completely, colliding with the winger's ankle. The sound of the impact silenced the crowd, the winger crumpling to the ground in pain. Alex froze, his eyes wide as the reality of what he'd done sank in.

The referee's whistle blew sharply, cutting through the tension. Alex didn't need to look up to know what was coming. The red card was raised high, and the referee pointed toward the tunnel. The crowd erupted, half in outrage, half in support, their voices a chaotic mix of jeers and applause.

Alex sat on the grass for a moment, his hands on his head, overwhelmed with guilt and regret. He wasn't just upset about the card—it was the sight of the rival player clutching his ankle, grimacing in pain, that hit him the hardest. He had meant to stop the attack, not hurt anyone. The weight of the injury felt heavier than the punishment.

Robin ran over, crouching beside Alex. "Come on, Alex," he said gently, his voice steady but filled with concern. "You've got to get up."

Alex shook his head, his voice cracking. "I didn't mean to hurt him, Robin. I just wanted to stop the play. I didn't–" He swallowed hard, the words catching in his throat.

Robin put a reassuring hand on his shoulder. "I know. We all know. But we've got to keep going. They'll take care of him."

Alex finally stood, his head hung low as the referee gestured for him to leave the field. As he walked toward the tunnel, the crowd's noise blurred into a dull hum in his ears. He glanced back at the injured player, now being helped up by the medics, and his chest tightened with a mix of shame and sympathy.

"I'm sorry," he whispered under his breath, though he knew the player couldn't hear him.

When Alex disappeared into the tunnel, Robin turned back to the rest of the team, who were regrouping with Coach Thompson on the sideline. The coach's face was set, a mix of frustration and determination. "We're down to ten now," he said firmly. "No more mistakes. Keep your shape, keep your heads, and work for each other."

Robin nodded, clapping his hands to rally his teammates. But in the back of his mind, he couldn't help but think about Alex, sitting alone in the changing room, carrying the weight of a moment's misjudgment. He would make sure to check on him after the game.

For now, there was still a battle to fight.

With just five minutes left, the rivals earned a free kick just outside the box. Their playmaker stepped up, curling the ball toward the top corner. Tommy, in a moment of brilliance, leapt and punched it away.

The team held their ground for the final moments, fighting tooth and nail to prevent another goal. The whistle blew, ending the match at 1-1.

As they walked off the pitch, the team was exhausted but proud. They had faced immense pressure and managed to hold their ground despite the challenges.

Coach Thompson gathered them for a quick talk, his tone firm but encouraging.

"This wasn't an easy game, and we made mistakes," he said, glancing at Alex, who nodded solemnly. "But we stuck together, and that's what matters. Learn from this, and let's keep building."

Robin looked around at his teammates, a sense of unity washing over him. They had faced their rivals and come out stronger for it. The season was far from over, but this match had shown them what they were capable of when they worked together.

The Importance of Sportsmanship

True greatness in soccer isn't just measured by goals but by the respect and integrity we show on and off the pitch·

The clubhouse was unusually quiet that evening. After their warm-up drills, Coach Thompson had gathered the team inside instead of heading to the training pitch. The boys sat on benches lining the room, their faces a mix of curiosity and apprehension. The mood was subdued— Alex sat at the far end, staring at his hands, his shoulders hunched. The memory of his red card and the injured opponent still weighed heavily on everyone.

Coach Thompson stood at the front of the room, arms crossed, his usual intensity replaced by a calm but serious demeanour. His voice was steady as he began, "Boys, we're not training tonight. There's something more important we need to talk about."

The team exchanged glances, the weight of the last match lingering in the air. Robin shifted uncomfortably, unsure of what to expect.

Coach took a deep breath, his gaze sweeping across the room. "Saturday's match was tough. You all played with determination, and I could see how much you wanted to win. But there was a moment in that game—something we need to address—because it goes beyond soccer."

All eyes turned toward Alex. He sat frozen, guilt etched across his face. The tackle that led to his red card and the opponent's injury replayed in his mind. He felt the weight of everyone's eyes, but no one said a word.

Coach took a step closer to Alex. "Alex," he said, his tone gentle but firm, "what happened on the pitch wasn't intentional. I know you didn't mean to hurt anyone. But we need to learn from this, not just for yourself but for the whole team."

Alex swallowed hard and finally looked up. "I didn't mean to hurt him, Coach. I was just trying to win the ball back. I…I feel awful about it."

Coach nodded. "I know you do. And that's why we're talking about this today. Soccer isn't just about skill or winning matches—it's about how we conduct ourselves, how we respect the game, our opponents, and each other."

Coach paused, letting his words sink in. "Let me tell you all a story—a true story about sportsmanship that the world remembers to this day."

The boys leaned in, curiosity piqued.

"In 2001, Paolo di Canio was playing for West Ham in the Premier League. During a match against Everton, their goalkeeper, Paul Gerrard, was injured. Di Canio had a chance to score—an open goal, no defenders in sight. But instead of taking the shot, he caught the ball with his hands and stopped the play so the goalkeeper could get help."

Robin's eyebrows shot up in surprise. "He didn't score?" he asked.

"No," Coach said with a small smile. "He didn't. But that act of sportsmanship made headlines around the world. People didn't remember that match for the scoreline—they remembered it for Di Canio's integrity. He put fairness above winning, and that's what made him a legend."

Alex shifted in his seat, his expression thoughtful. "Do you think people respected him more for that?"

"Absolutely," Coach said. "Di Canio once said, 'Winning without respect is like scoring without the joy.' And he was right. Soccer is about more than just goals—it's about the values we show on the pitch."

Coach turned to the whole team now. "Boys, I want you to think about what kind of players—and people—you want to be. It's easy to get caught up in the heat of the game, to let emotions take over. But the true test of character comes in those moments. Do we lash out, or do we stay composed? Do we win at any cost, or do we play with integrity?"

He began pacing slowly. "Sportsmanship is what makes soccer more than just a game. It's about respect—respect for the sport, for your opponents, for your teammates, and for yourself. And respect isn't just shown when we win—it's shown in how we handle failure, frustration, and even success."

Robin nodded, the words resonating deeply. He thought back to the games where he had been frustrated but had kept his composure, knowing it mattered not just to him but to his team.

Coach turned back to Alex. "Alex, you made a mistake, and that's okay. Mistakes are part of the game. What matters now is how you respond. The player you tackled is recovering, and I think it would mean a lot if you reached out to him, maybe apologise."

Alex hesitated, guilt flickering across his face. "Do you think he'd even want to hear from me?"

"I do," Coach said firmly. "Apologising shows strength, not weakness. It shows that you care and that you're willing to take responsibility. That's the kind of player—and person—you want to be."

Alex nodded slowly. "I'll do it," he said, his voice quiet but resolute. "I'll reach out."

Coach stepped back, addressing the entire team. "This season, we're focusing on defending. And that doesn't just mean defending the goal—it means defending the values of the game. Every time you step onto that pitch, remember that you represent more than just yourselves. You represent your teammates, your club, and this sport we all love."

He paused, his gaze sweeping the room. "Winning is important, but how you play the game is what people will remember."

The team sat in silence for a moment, each player reflecting on what Coach had said. Then Robin spoke up. "I think we all have moments where we let the game get to us. But maybe if we support each other more, we can make sure we stay focused on what really matters."

Coach smiled. "Well said, Robin. Supporting each other is what makes us strong. And that's what I expect from all of you—not just skill and effort, but respect and integrity."

The boys nodded in agreement, a renewed sense of purpose filling the room. As they left the clubhouse, Alex felt a small weight lift from his shoulders. He wasn't defined by his mistake—he was defined by how he chose to move forward. And with his teammates by his side, he knew he could make things right.

Compactness in 4-3-3

*A tight defence is more than positioning—it's the
heartbeat of a disciplined team.*

The golden afternoon sun cast long shadows over the training ground as Robin and his teammates jogged onto the pitch. The air was filled with a renewed sense of determination after the previous intense sessions on sportsmanship and discipline. Today, the focus was shifting back to tactics, and Coach Thompson had promised an introduction to one of soccer's most effective defensive formations: the 4-3-3.

Robin's curiosity was piqued. He knew that their defensive struggles in recent matches highlighted the need for improvement. The mood was lighter, though, with the occasional burst of laughter and banter from his teammates.

Coach Thompson blew his whistle, calling everyone into a semicircle. His tone was steady but enthusiastic. "Alright, team, today we're diving into compactness in the 4-3-3 formation. It's not just about defending—it's about controlling the game, denying space, and preparing for quick transitions. Done right, it's one of the most balanced systems in soccer."

Jake, ever the joker, raised his hand with exaggerated seriousness. "So, Coach, does this mean I'll finally get a chance to score more goals?"

The group erupted in laughter, and Coach shook his head, smirking. "Only if you press well and win the ball back, Jake. No shortcuts here."

Jake nudged Robin with a grin. "Guess I'll have to do your job too, mate."

Robin rolled his eyes, chuckling. "Just don't lose the ball up front, and we'll be fine."

Coach stepped in, tapping his whiteboard with a marker. "Enough jokes. Let's break this down."

Coach Thompson's voice was firm as he began his explanation. "Compactness means staying tight as a team—no unnecessary gaps, either horizontally or vertically. When we defend, we aim to force the opposition wide or backward. Denying space forces mistakes."

He pointed to the board, which displayed the 4-3-3 formation. "The back four stays narrow, communicating constantly. The midfield three shields the defence and cuts off passing lanes, while the forwards press high to disrupt the opposition's buildup."

Alex tilted his head, considering. "So, it's like squeezing them into a box where they can't breathe?"

"Exactly," Coach replied. "But it only works if everyone stays disciplined. One weak link and the whole structure collapses."

The players nodded, soaking in the lesson. Robin, standing next to Alex, felt a sense of clarity. The explanation was simple but powerful, and he could already picture the shape on the pitch.

Coach divided the players into two groups: defenders in the 4-3-3 shape and attackers trying to break them down. Robin was slotted into the defensive midfield role and tasked with organising the team.

The first attempt was chaotic. The attackers found gaps easily, slipping through with quick passes. Robin shouted instructions, but communication among the defenders faltered.

Coach blew his whistle sharply. "Stop! Reset. Robin, good job directing traffic, but midfield, you're too spread out. Stay closer to the backline and cut those passing lanes."

On the second attempt, Robin kept his midfielders tighter. He called out constantly, "Jake, block the left! Ollie, watch your spacing!" The attackers struggled to penetrate the compact shape. Alex read a pass perfectly, intercepting it with a quick touch and clearing it wide.

Coach clapped his hands. "That's it! Stay tight and deny space. Great work, Alex!"

Robin felt the team's confidence growing. The drill was challenging, but they were beginning to see the benefits of compactness.

The next drill focused on transitioning from defence to attack. Coach split the field into three zones—defence, midfield, and attack—and tasked the defending team with winning the ball in their zone and launching a counterattack within three passes.

Jake, as usual, couldn't resist a bit of fun. "Ready to see me score again, Robin?"

Robin smirked. "If you can stay onside, maybe."

The first attempt was promising. Alex intercepted a pass, feeding the ball to Robin, who turned swiftly and spotted Jake sprinting down the right. Robin sent a perfectly weighted through-ball into space. Jake latched onto it and slotted it into the net with ease.

"Told you I'd score!" Jake shouted, grinning.

Robin laughed. "You should thank me for that pass!"

The next attempt didn't go as smoothly. Ollie tried to dribble out of defence and was dispossessed by a pressing attacker. The opposition quickly capitalised, scoring a goal. Alex groaned in frustration. "Sorry, guys, I should've been quicker to close him down."

Coach nodded. "Mistakes happen, Alex. What's important is how fast we recover. You'll get it next time."

The drill resumed, and this time, the team executed the transition flawlessly. Robin intercepted a pass and immediately launched it to Ollie, who broke down the wing and delivered a cross to Jake for a clean finish.

The final drill of the day was designed to test their compactness under pressure. Coach set up a 5v5 game in a smaller area of the pitch. The defenders had to maintain their shape and prevent the attackers from creating clear chances.

Robin's voice rang out across the pitch. "Alex, step up! Ollie, don't leave that gap open!" The attackers pressed hard, attempting quick one-twos to break through the compact shape, but the defenders stayed organised.

At one point, Jake broke free and fired a shot toward the corner, but Tommy made an acrobatic save, diving low to tip the ball away. "Great save, Tommy!" Robin shouted.

"Thanks, mate!" Tommy replied, grinning.

The drill ended with the defenders holding their shape, forcing the attackers to take desperate, low-percentage shots. Coach gathered the team for a debrief.

As the players stretched on the grass, Jake nudged Robin. "Not bad for a defensive clinic, eh?"

Robin smirked. "Let's see if you remember all this in the next game."

Coach Thompson called everyone into a circle. "Great work today, team. Compactness isn't just about defending—it's about discipline and unity. You're making progress, but remember, it takes constant focus to get it right. We'll test it in the next match."

The players nodded, their confidence growing. Robin felt ready to put everything they had practised into action. As the sun dipped below the horizon, he couldn't help but feel excited for the challenges ahead.

Resilient and Ruthless

Victory tastes sweetest when it's earned through grit, precision, and teamwork.

The hum of excitement buzzed through the changing room as Robin tied his laces. Around him, his teammates chatted, their voices filled with nervous energy and anticipation. Jake, as usual, was the loudest.

"Today's the day, lads," Jake said, standing and striking a mock superhero pose. "Hat-trick incoming. I can feel it."

Ollie smirked from the other side of the room. "Hat-trick of missed shots, maybe."

Laughter rippled through the team as Jake clutched his chest in mock offence. "Ollie, my boy, you wound me."

Robin grinned but stayed focused, recalling Coach Thompson's words from training. Compact defence, smart transitions, and discipline—those were the keys to today's match.

Coach entered, silencing the chatter instantly. His presence commanded attention. "Alright, team, listen up." He stood in the centre of the room, his voice calm but firm. "We've trained for this. We've talked about compactness, about transitions, about staying disciplined. Now's the time to show it."

He paused, looking around the room, making eye contact with each player. "Robin, Alex, Ollie—this game is about working as a unit. You've all shown how much you've grown, but today, we take it to the next level. Deny them space. Force mistakes. And when we get the ball, we move fast. No hesitation."

The team nodded, their confidence rising with every word. Coach's belief in them was infectious.

"Alright," Coach finished, clapping his hands. "Get out there and show them what we're made of."

The whistle blew, and the game began. The opposition came out aggressively, pressing high and testing Robin's team's defensive organisation. But Robin, playing as a defensive midfielder, was ready.

The first real test came in the 12th minute. An opposition winger sprinted down the left flank, looking to cut inside. Alex, positioned perfectly, anticipated the move and stepped up with a clean-standing tackle. The ball ricocheted to Robin, who quickly assessed his options.

"Jake! Wide!" Robin shouted, sending a long diagonal pass to Ollie on the wing. The transition was seamless.

Ollie darted forward, his speed leaving defenders in his wake. He crossed the ball into the box, where Jake leapt to meet it with a powerful header.

The net bulged. 1-0.

The team erupted in cheers, rushing to celebrate with Jake. "Told you!" Jake shouted, grinning ear to ear.

Robin gave him a high-five. "Nice one. Just don't let it go to your head."

The opposition, undeterred by the early goal, stepped up their game. Their midfielders began to probe for gaps, moving the ball quickly and testing the team's compactness. Robin barked instructions, his voice cutting through the noise.

"Alex, shift left! Ollie, drop back!"

The pressure mounted as the opposition's right winger delivered a dangerous cross into the box. Tommy, their goalkeeper, shouted, "Mine!" as he leapt to punch the ball clear. The rebound fell to an opposition midfielder, who fired a shot toward the goal.

Alex threw himself in front of the ball, blocking it with his chest and sending it out for a corner. He winced slightly but quickly got back to his feet, earning a round of applause from his teammates.

"Great block, Alex!" Robin shouted, clapping his hands.

As the first half wore on, the opposition grew more desperate, and Robin's team began to lose a bit of focus. In the 42nd minute, a lapse in communication between Alex and Ollie left a gap in the defensive line. The opposition's striker pounced, receiving a perfectly timed through-ball and finding himself one-on-one with Tommy.

Tommy rushed off his line, trying to close the angle, but the striker remained composed, slotting the ball into the bottom corner. The opposition celebrated as Robin's team stood in silence, the sting of the mistake weighing on them.

Back in the changing room, the mood was sombre. The players slumped in their seats, frustration etched on their faces. Robin stared at the floor, replaying the mistake in his mind.

Coach Thompson walked in, his expression calm but serious. "Alright, listen up," he began, his tone firm but encouraging. "We're tied, but that's no reason to hang your heads. Mistakes happen. What matters is how we respond."

He pointed at Alex and Ollie. "You two, better communication next time. Talk to each other. Robin, keep leading from the midfield. You've been solid, but I need you to push harder."

Then, his voice softened. "We've got 45 minutes to make this game ours. Stay compact. Stay disciplined. And when you get the ball, transition fast. Trust each other."

Jake, always one to lighten the mood, piped up. "And trust me to score again."

Laughter broke the tension, and the team's spirits lifted. Robin felt a renewed sense of determination. They weren't done yet.

"Alright," Coach said, clapping his hands. "Let's go out there and finish this."

The whistle blew to start the second half, and Robin's team immediately showed renewed energy. The words of Coach Thompson rang in Robin's ears: *Stay compact. Transition fast.*

The opposition, buoyed by their late first-half goal, pushed forward aggressively. Their striker tried to exploit gaps in the defence, but Robin and Alex were ready.

In the 48th minute, the opposition's right-winger attempted to dribble past Ollie. This time, Ollie held his ground, timing his tackle perfectly. The ball spilt loose, and Robin swooped in to recover it. He immediately turned and sent a sharp pass to Jake, who had dropped deep to support.

"Let's move!" Robin shouted, sprinting forward to join the attack. Jake spotted Ollie making a run on the right wing and fed him the ball. With his speed, Ollie reached the byline and sent a dangerous low cross into the box. The opposition's defender managed to clear it, but the warning was clear—Robin's team was back in the fight.

As the game settled into a rhythm, Robin's team demonstrated their growing defensive discipline. In the 55th minute, the opposition launched a quick counterattack. Their attacking midfielder dribbled at speed, trying to bypass the midfield line. Robin anticipated the move, cutting off his path with a sharp interception.

"Alex, cover me!" Robin shouted as he passed the ball back to Tommy to reset the play. Tommy, calm and collected, rolled the ball out to Ollie on the wing.

The opposition pressed hard, but the back four stayed compact and composed. Alex and the other defenders communicated constantly, keeping their line tight and denying space. The opposition resorted to long balls, which were easily dealt with by Tommy and the defenders.

In the 60th minute, the opposition managed to get a shot off from distance. The ball was heading for the top corner, but Tommy leapt spectacularly, tipping it over the bar. The crowd erupted into applause as his teammates rushed to congratulate him.

"Great save, Tommy!" Alex shouted, patting him on the back.

Tommy grinned. "Just doing my job."

In the 67th minute, the opposition pushed high up the pitch, leaving themselves vulnerable to a counterattack. Robin spotted the opportunity and intercepted a risky pass in midfield. Without hesitation, he turned and sent a quick, long ball to Jake, who was already on the move.

Jake controlled it with a deft touch, sprinting toward goal with only one defender to beat. Ollie darted into the box, drawing the defender away and leaving Jake with a clear path. Jake kept his composure and fired a low shot past the goalkeeper.

The net rippled. 2-1.

Jake sprinted toward the corner flag, arms outstretched in celebration. "That's two for me!" he shouted, laughing.

Robin jogged over, shaking his head with a grin. "You're welcome for the pass."

The opposition, now trailing, threw everything into attack. Their desperation led to mistakes, and Robin's team capitalised. In the 75th minute, Alex cleared a dangerous cross out of the box, and Robin picked up the loose ball. He quickly played it wide to Ollie, who sprinted down the wing.

Ollie cut inside, evading two defenders, and sent a lofted cross into the box. Jake leapt high, nodding the ball toward the goal. The goalkeeper parried it, but Ollie followed up, smashing the rebound into the roof of the net.

3-1.

The players celebrated wildly, their confidence surging. Coach Thompson clapped from the sidelines, shouting encouragement. "Great teamwork! Keep it tight now!"

With ten minutes left, Robin's team kept their defensive shape, forcing the opposition into errors. In the 85th minute, Alex intercepted a poorly executed pass, sending a long ball to Ollie on the counter.

Ollie, brimming with confidence, dribbled past two defenders and slipped a pass to Jake, who was waiting at the edge of the box. Instead of shooting, Jake unselfishly laid the ball off to Robin, who had made a late run into the box.

Robin struck the ball first-time, sending it soaring into the top corner. The goalkeeper didn't even move. 4-1.

The team rushed to Robin, cheering loudly. Jake grinned and slapped Robin on the back. "About time you got on the score sheet."

Robin laughed, the joy of the moment washing over him. "Couldn't let you have all the fun."

The final whistle blew, and the game ended with a resounding 4-1 victory. The players hugged and high-fived, their hard work paying off in a dominating performance.

Coach Thompson gathered them on the pitch for a quick debrief. "That was outstanding. You stayed compact, defended as a unit, and transitioned brilliantly. This is what we've been working toward."

He looked around at the beaming faces of his players. "Remember this feeling. This is what happens when we trust the system and work for each other."

As they headed off the pitch, Robin felt a deep sense of satisfaction. It wasn't just about the win—it was about the journey they had taken together to get there. And this was just the beginning.

Versatility in 3-5-2

Flexibility in tactics isn't just an advantage—it's the key to unlocking potential.

The sun was warm, but a slight breeze cooled the training ground as Robin and his teammates gathered on the pitch. Spirits were high after their commanding 4-1 victory, but the reflection in the locker room earlier had been sobering. They all knew that football wasn't just about one good game—it was about building consistency.

Coach Thompson, as always, was one step ahead. He stood at the edge of the pitch, clipboard in hand, a faint smile on his face. Robin could tell he had something planned.

"Alright, team," Coach called, motioning for them to gather. As the players jogged over, he continued, "Let's talk about that win. You played brilliantly—compact, focused, and quick to transition. But as proud as I am of you, remember this: the next game is always the most important. Today, we're going to focus on something new."

Ollie nudged Robin. "New formation? Maybe we're playing with two keepers this time," he whispered, grinning.

Robin chuckled. "Or maybe we'll let Jake try defending."

Jake overheard and puffed out his chest. "Hey, I'd be a great defender! I'd just tackle everyone, problem solved."

The group laughed, and even Coach cracked a smile. "Glad to see you're all in good spirits because today, we're learning the 3-5-2 formation."

The players exchanged glances, intrigued. Coach pulled out a whiteboard and began sketching. "The 3-5-2 is a versatile formation. It gives us strength in defence, control in midfield, and options in attack. But it requires discipline. Let me break it down."

Coach pointed at the board. "Here's how it works. Three central defenders form the backbone—tight, compact, and always communicating. The midfield five are the key. Wing-backs provide width, while the central three manage the game, transitioning between defence and attack. Up front, two strikers work together to press and create chances."

Alex raised his hand. "And what about when we lose the ball? Does everyone drop back?"

Coach nodded. "Good question. The midfield has to shift quickly, covering spaces while the wing-backs trackback. If one defender steps out, the others close ranks. It's all about working as a unit."

Robin was assigned the central midfield role, with Ollie as the left wing-back and Alex in central defence. Jake, of course, was one of the strikers. As they took their positions on the field, Coach reminded them, "This formation works only if everyone communicates. No lone wolves out here."

Coach set up the first drill to test their compactness. The defenders and midfielders had to hold their shape against an attacking team that was trying to exploit gaps. Robin stood in the heart of midfield, ready to direct traffic.

"Alright, let's go!" Coach shouted, and the attackers sprang into action.

The first attempt was chaotic. The attackers found space on the wings, and Alex stepped out of position, leaving a gap in the centre. A quick pass sliced through, and the attackers scored easily.

Coach blew his whistle. "Stop! What happened there?"

Robin turned to Alex. "You went too wide. Stay closer to the other defenders."

Alex nodded, looking determined. "Got it. Let's try again."

This time, the defenders stayed compact. When the attackers tried to push through the centre, Robin intercepted the ball and cleared it. "That's it!" Coach called. "Good work. Keep talking to each other."

The drill continued, and the team gradually improved. Ollie tracked back when needed, Alex held his ground, and Robin kept the midfield organised. By the end of the drill, the attackers were struggling to find space.

Coach transitioned to the next drill, focusing on the midfield. "In the 3-5-2, midfielders are the glue. You need to balance defence and attack, covering for the wing-backs when they push forward."

Robin's group was tasked with maintaining possession in a small-sided game. The wing-backs joined in, simulating support on the flanks.

"Think fast!" Coach yelled as the drill began. The attackers pressed aggressively, and Robin found himself surrounded. He shielded the ball, looked up, and passed it to Ollie, who overlapped on the wing.

"Go, Ollie!" Robin shouted. Ollie sprinted forward, crossing the ball to Jake, who volleyed it into the net. "That's how it's done!" Jake yelled, grinning.

But the next attempt wasn't as smooth. Ollie lost the ball while trying to dribble out of defence, and the attackers capitalised, scoring easily. Alex groaned. "We've got to be quicker on the transition."

Coach nodded. "Exactly. Win the ball, look up, and make a decision. Robin, you're doing well, but keep scanning for those quick outlets."

The drill continued, and the team began to find their rhythm. Robin anchored the midfield, making quick passes and directing play. Ollie adjusted his positioning, staying ready to defend when needed. By the end, the team had improved significantly, and even Coach looked pleased.

As the players gathered for a quick water break, the camaraderie was evident. Jake teased Ollie about his dribbling mishap, and Robin couldn't resist chiming in. "You're supposed to pass, not audition for a highlight reel."

Ollie grinned. "Hey, I like to keep it exciting."

Coach clapped his hands, drawing their attention. "Great work so far. The 3-5-2 is challenging, but you're getting the hang of it. Let's keep building on this. In the next session, we'll focus on how to transition from this setup into the attack."

The team nodded, their confidence growing. Robin felt a renewed sense of purpose. The 3-5-2 was tough to master, but with each drill, they were getting closer.

Coach Thompson brought out cones to set up zones on the field. "Now, we'll work on transitioning from defence to attack in the 3-5-2. Defenders, midfielders, and forwards—pay attention to how quickly you can adapt."

Robin's team began in a defensive setup, with the attackers trying to break through. Tommy, in goal, made a fantastic save, diving to his left. As the defenders regrouped, Robin shouted, "Ollie, wide! Alex, push up!"

Tommy quickly rolled the ball to Robin, who spun and threaded a pass to Jake. Jake, in sync with the midfield's movement, sprinted forward. Robin followed up, supporting the attack. Jake flicked the ball back to Robin, who sent a perfectly weighted pass to the overlapping Ollie.

Ollie crossed the ball into the box, where Jake volleyed it into the net. "Beautiful!" Coach Thompson cheered. "That's how you transition–fast, precise, and decisive."

The next round wasn't as smooth. Alex stepped too far out of position, leaving a gap the attackers exploited. Tommy saved the first shot, but the rebound went in. Alex groaned. "I got pulled out again."

Robin clapped his shoulder. "It's alright. Just stay closer to us next time. We'll cover if you need to step out."

The drills continued, with the team gradually improving their coordination and speed. By the end, they had found a rhythm, seamlessly transitioning from defence to attack.

As the session wound down, Coach Thompson gathered the players in a circle. "Great effort today, everyone. The 3-5-2 is not easy–it demands versatility and discipline. But you're making progress."

Robin wiped the sweat from his brow, nodding. He could feel the difference with each drill. The formation was challenging but rewarding when executed correctly.

Coach continued, his tone encouraging. "Remember, every player has a role to play in this system. Defenders must stay compact, midfielders need to adapt quickly, and forwards must press and finish efficiently. It's all about working together."

Jake grinned. "And scoring goals. Let's not forget that part."

The team laughed, and even Coach chuckled. "Yes, Jake, scoring goals is important. But it starts with strong defending and smart transitions."

Robin exchanged smiles with Ollie and Alex. The drills had been tough, but they'd learned a lot about how to function as a unit. He felt ready to take on the challenge of implementing the 3-5-2 in a real game.

As they packed up their gear, Ollie turned to Robin. "Think we'll nail this formation in a match?"

Robin shrugged with a grin. "Only if Jake remembers to press instead of just waiting to score."

Jake rolled his eyes. "You'll miss me when I'm scoring hat-tricks."

Coach Thompson clapped his hands. "Alright, everyone, good work today. Next session, we'll refine this further. Get some rest–you've earned it."

The players headed off the pitch, joking and laughing as they walked. Robin felt a sense of camaraderie growing stronger with each session. They weren't just learning tactics–they were becoming a team that could rely on each other, no matter the challenge.

A Day Off at Robin's Home

Friendships off the pitch build the trust needed to win on it.

The smell of freshly baked cookies filled the air as Robin helped his mum arrange snacks in the kitchen. The house was buzzing with energy in anticipation of his friends arriving. His dad had already set up the gaming console in the living room, giving Robin a thumbs-up before retreating to his workshop.

"Do you think we have enough snacks?" Robin asked, glancing at the bowls of crisps, cookies, and popcorn.

His mum laughed. "If your friends eat like you do, I'm not sure we'll ever have enough."

The doorbell rang, and Robin rushed to answer it, greeted by Jake, who was predictably late. "Took your time, didn't you?" Robin teased.

Jake grinned, holding up a bag of sweets. "I bring gifts. That should make up for it."

One by one, the rest of the team arrived. Ollie strutted in, proudly showing off his new haircut. "Freshest cut on the team," he declared, earning groans and playful shoves from the others.

Tommy carried a book on tactical formations under his arm, causing Jake to groan. "Mate, it's a day off. You're not seriously bringing homework, are you?"

"It's not homework," Tommy replied, rolling his eyes. "It's research."

Robin welcomed Alex last, who showed up with a small portable speaker. "For atmosphere," he explained, setting it down as music filled the room.

The boys settled in the living room, gathering around the gaming console. The screen lit up with a popular soccer video game, and chaos ensued as everyone clamoured to pick their teams.

"I call dibs on the national champions!" Jake shouted, grabbing the controller.

Robin shoved him lightly. "Not so fast. You had them last time."

After a few rounds of playful arguing, the teams were set. Jake, predictably, played with aggression, yelling instructions at his digital players. Ollie, to everyone's surprise, showcased unexpected skill, weaving through defenders and scoring a stunning goal.

"Did you see that?" Ollie exclaimed, throwing his hands in the air. "I'm a natural."

Jake groaned, leaning back on the couch. "Beginner's luck."

Alex, usually quiet, leaned forward with focus, pulling off a perfect tactical move in the next round. "Maybe you should stick to drama, Jake," he teased.

The room filled with laughter as Jake threw a cushion at Alex. Even Tommy, usually serious, couldn't hide his grin. "If only you could execute plays like this in real life," Tommy quipped.

"Careful," Robin interjected with a smirk. "We wouldn't want to hurt Jake's feelings."

After a few intense matches, the boys paused for snacks. They sprawled around the room, talking about life outside soccer.

"So, what's everyone up to outside of football?" Robin asked, breaking the silence.

Jake grinned. "You'll never guess. I'm auditioning for a school play next week."

"What?!" Ollie almost choked on his popcorn. "Since when are you into drama?"

Jake shrugged. "Since Miss Harding said I had 'natural charisma.'"

"You mean a big mouth," Alex joked, earning a round of laughter.

Alex shared his own story next. "I've been working on a new piece for piano. Played it at a recital last weekend. Forgot the sheet music but made it through somehow."

"Improvisation—always handy," Robin said. "That's the musician's version of a last-minute save."

Tommy spoke next, his eyes lighting up. "I'm entering a science competition. Building a model of a solar-powered drone. It's been fun, but it's a lot of work."

The group listened, impressed by Tommy's ambition. "You'll have to let us know when it's done," Robin said. "We'll come see it in action."

Finally, Robin admitted, "I've been reading loads of mystery novels. Can't get enough of them."

Jake smirked. "Detective Robin. Maybe you can solve the case of why I keep beating you in this game."

Robin tossed a cushion at him. "In your dreams."

Robin's mum called the boys to the dining table, where a spread of homemade pizza awaited. They crowded around, helping themselves while keeping the conversation lively.

"Alright," Jake said, his mouth full. "Let's talk dreams. Where do you see yourself in five years?"

"I'll be a professional footballer and an actor," Jake declared, earning another round of groans.

"You can't be both," Alex pointed out.

"Watch me," Jake replied confidently.

Alex shared that he hoped to pursue music while keeping soccer in his life. Tommy talked about how soccer had taught him teamwork, which he wanted to apply to engineering projects.

Robin's dad chimed in with a story about his own youth. "I tried to play soccer once. Scored an own goal in my first match."

The table erupted in laughter as Robin's mum shook her head. "He's not exaggerating. It's why he's better in the garden than on the pitch."

As the evening wound down, the boys gathered in Robin's room, sprawled across the bed and floor. They talked about the season so far and what lay ahead.

"We've got a lot to work on," Tommy said. "But I think we're getting better."

"Definitely," Alex agreed. "That last game showed how far we've come."

Jake grinned. "And how far we still have to go. No more own goals, Robin."

Robin laughed, shaking his head. "That was your mistake, not mine."

The boys made a pact to support each other, not just on the field but in everything they did. "We're a team, on and off the pitch," Robin said, and the others nodded.

As they left for the night, Robin stood at the door, watching his friends walk down the driveway. The house was quieter now, but the warmth of the evening lingered.

He smiled, thinking about the journey ahead. They were more than just teammates—they were family.

Defending Set Pieces

In moments of stillness, strength and strategy reveal themselves·

The afternoon sun cast long shadows over the pitch as Robin and his teammates jogged onto the field for their weekly training session. After the excitement and challenges of their recent games, Coach Thompson had promised a day dedicated to mastering a critical part of soccer: defending set pieces. Robin knew this was an area where their team could improve, and he felt a mix of anticipation and determination.

Coach Thompson blew his whistle, gathering the team in a semicircle near the whiteboard. His voice carried authority but also a note of encouragement. "Alright, team, let's talk about set pieces," he began, pointing to diagrams of different defensive setups. "These moments—corners, free kicks, throw-ins—are some of the most decisive in a game. A single lapse in focus can cost us dearly."

Jake, always ready with a joke, raised his hand. "So, Coach, if I just don't defend during corners, does that mean I can focus on scoring instead?"

Laughter rippled through the group, and Coach shook his head, smirking. "Only if you want to be benched for the next game, Jake."

Robin nudged Jake playfully. "Or if you want to hear Tommy yelling at you for the rest of the season."

Tommy grinned from his spot near the goal. "You got that right."

Coach clapped his hands, bringing them back to focus. "Let's break it down. Today, we're working on corners, free kicks, throw-ins, and even penalties. It's all about organisation, communication, and discipline."

Coach Thompson started with corners, sketching a simple defensive setup on his whiteboard. "There are two main approaches to defending corners: man-to-man marking and zonal marking. Man-to-man means each of you is responsible for an opposing player. You stick to them like glue. Zonal marking, on the other hand, means you're protecting a specific area of the box."

Robin raised his hand. "Which one are we using, Coach?"

"We'll practice both," Coach replied. "Man-to-man is great for staying tight on their key players, but zonal marking can help us cover dangerous spaces. The key is to be disciplined no matter which system we use."

Alex leaned in, his brow furrowed. "What if they mix it up? You know, overload one side?"

Coach nodded approvingly. "Good question, Alex. That's why communication is crucial. If you see an overload, shout it out and shift your positions accordingly. Now, let's take it to the field."

The team split into attackers and defenders. Robin's group took on the defensive role, lining up in the box as Jake and the attacking group prepared to take corners. Coach Thompson stood on the sidelines, observing closely.

"Robin, you're in the middle, organising the back line," Coach called out. "Keep your eyes on the ball and your teammates."

As the first corner came in, chaos erupted. Jake's delivery was sharp, and Ollie darted toward the near post. Robin shouted, "Stay tight! Watch your man!" but Alex lost his marker, and Ollie's header sailed just over the bar.

Coach blew his whistle. "Stop! Reset!" He jogged over to the group. "Alex, what happened there?"

Alex sighed. "I got caught ball-watching."

Coach nodded. "It happens. But remember, in man-to-man marking, your job is your player. The ball comes second."

The next attempt went better. Robin stayed vocal, guiding Alex to stay close to his man. When the cross came in, Robin cleared it with a strong header, earning a nod of approval from Coach.

"That's more like it," Coach said. "Stay focused, stay organised."

The team shifted to defending free kicks, with Tommy arranging the wall and Coach setting up different scenarios. Robin took a spot near the edge of the box, ready to track runners.

Coach explained, "For wide free kicks, it's about defending the second ball. The first header might not always clear it, so stay alert for rebounds."

The whistle blew, and Jake curled in a dangerous delivery. Robin tracked Alex, who was his assigned man this time, ensuring he couldn't make a run toward the goal. The ball was headed out, but it fell to Ollie at the edge of the box. He struck it cleanly, forcing Tommy into a diving save.

"Nice one, Tommy!" Robin shouted as Tommy scrambled to his feet.

The next free kick presented a tougher challenge. Jake faked a shot, then lofted the ball over the wall. The attackers surged forward, and it was Alex who made a critical interception, clearing the ball under pressure. "That's it, Alex!" Robin called out, patting him on the back.

Coach Thompson set up a smaller drill for defending throw-ins near the box. "Throw-ins can seem harmless, but if we switch off, they can create dangerous chances," he explained.

Robin positioned himself near the centre, watching as Ollie prepared to take a long throw. The ball flew into the box, and for a moment, it looked like Jake might get on the end of it. But Robin timed his jump perfectly, clearing the danger with a strong header.

Jake grinned as they reset. "You're ruining all my fun, Robin."

Robin smirked. "That's kind of the point, Jake."

The session wrapped up with a penalty defence. Tommy stood tall in goal, facing each teammate one by one as they stepped up to take their shots. Robin noticed Tommy's focus, his eyes locked on the taker's movements.

Coach paused to share a story. "There was a famous goalkeeper, Lev Yashin, who was known for saving penalties. He said, 'The joy of seeing Yuri Gagarin flying in space is only superseded by the joy of a good penalty save.' Tommy, channel your inner Yashin."

Tommy laughed but took the advice seriously. As Jake stepped up to take a penalty, Tommy guessed correctly, diving to his right and pushing the ball away. The team erupted in cheers.

As the session wound down, the players gathered around Coach for a final debrief. "Today, we worked on something that can make or break a game," Coach said. "Set pieces are about discipline, focus, and teamwork. You showed great progress, but remember—one lapse, and it can cost us."

Robin reflected on the drills, feeling more confident in his understanding of set-piece defence. The team's camaraderie was growing stronger, and with it, their ability to work as a unit.

As they walked off the pitch, Jake nudged Robin. "Think we'll see these drills in the next game?"

Robin grinned. "Definitely. And this time, we'll be ready."

The Final Game

The true measure of a team is not in how it starts,
but in how it finishes·

The locker room was alive with energy as the players sat on the wooden benches, adjusting their boots and pulling up their socks. This was it—the final game of the season. The culmination of months of hard work, drills, and endless conversations about tactics. Robin felt the familiar blend of nerves and excitement coursing through him as he glanced around at his teammates, their expressions ranging from focused to quietly determined.

Coach Thompson stood at the centre of the room, a clipboard in hand and a fire in his eyes. His presence alone was enough to quiet the murmurs and laughter. "Alright, team," he began, his voice steady but brimming with conviction, "this is it. Everything we've practised, everything we've talked about—today is the day to bring it all together."

Coach set his clipboard down on the bench and stepped forward, his gaze meeting each player's eyes. "Let's talk about what we've achieved this season," he said, pacing slowly. "When we started, we were a team full of potential but lacking structure. Now look at us. We've mastered defensive formations, learned how to transition from defence to attack, and built a bond that makes us more than just a team—we're a unit."

Jake leaned back, a confident grin on his face. "So, we're basically unstoppable, right?"

Coach chuckled. "If you remember everything we've worked on, yes. But only if you keep your focus. Today, I want you to think about all the key elements we've practised: compactness, pressing, marking, and set-piece defence. This game is the perfect opportunity to show how far we've come."

Robin raised his hand, his expression serious. "What's the game plan, Coach?"

Coach nodded, stepping over to his clipboard. "We're starting in a 4-3-3. Our focus in the first half is high pressing and quick transitions. I want the forwards and midfielders to stay tight, win the ball early, and hit them on the counter. Stay compact, stay disciplined, and communicate."

He paused, letting his words sink in before continuing. "But remember, it's not just about defence. When you have the ball, be creative, be bold. Use the space and take your chances. This is your time to shine."

The players exchanged nods, their confidence growing with each word. Tommy, their goalkeeper, punched his gloves together. "Let's do this."

Coach stepped back, his tone softening. "Remember, this game isn't just about the scoreline. It's about showing yourself what you're capable of. Play for each other, enjoy the game, and leave everything out there on the pitch."

With that, Coach clapped his hands. "Alright, team, let's go!"

The roar of the crowd greeted Robin and his teammates as they stepped onto the field. The sun was shining, and the pitch was in perfect condition–a fitting stage for their final challenge. Robin took his position in midfield, glancing back at the defensive line and forward at Jake, who was already pacing near the opposition's box.

The whistle blew, and the game began with a burst of energy. Robin's team pressed high, just as Coach had instructed. Within minutes, the pressure paid off. Alex intercepted a pass near the halfway line and immediately played it forward to Robin, who turned sharply and spotted Ollie making a run down the right flank.

"Ollie, go!" Robin shouted, sending a perfectly weighted pass into space. Ollie sprinted onto the ball, beat his marker with a quick feint, and crossed it into the box. Jake was there, rising above the defenders to head the ball into the net.

1-0.

The crowd erupted, and Jake turned to Robin, grinning. "Told you I'd score first."

Robin laughed, clapping him on the back. "You better keep it up."

The early goal seemed to energise the team even more. Robin's midfield trio worked tirelessly, cutting off passing lanes and launching quick counterattacks. The opposition struggled to find their rhythm, their frustration evident in their rushed passes and heavy touches.

Ten minutes later, Robin found himself in possession again. He dribbled past an advancing midfielder and spotted Alex making a late run into the box. With a quick flick, Robin threaded the ball through the defence. Alex took a touch and fired it past the goalkeeper.

2-0.

The team celebrated together, their camaraderie on full display. Coach Thompson clapped from the sideline, his voice carrying above the cheers. "That's it! Stay compact, keep the pressure on!"

As the first half wore on, the opposition tried to push back, but Robin's team held their shape. Tommy made a crucial save off a long-range effort, and the defenders cleared the subsequent corner with authority. Every player seemed to be in sync, their movements fluid and purposeful.

With just minutes left in the half, Robin won the ball near the centre circle and immediately launched a counterattack. He played a quick one-two with Ollie before sending a lofted pass over the defence to Jake. Jake controlled it with his chest, took a step forward, and smashed it into the net.

3-0.

The referee's whistle blew for halftime, and the team jogged back to the changing room, their spirits soaring. Robin couldn't help but smile as he looked around at his teammates. They were playing some of their best soccer yet, and he knew they were making Coach proud.

In the locker room, the atmosphere was electric. Coach Thompson stood in front of the team, his expression a mix of pride and focus. "You're doing brilliantly out there," he said. "Three goals up, and you've shown exactly what we've worked on all season. Compact defending, quick transitions, and clinical finishing."

He paused, letting the players take it in. "But remember, the game isn't over. The second half is where champions are made. Stay disciplined, stay sharp, and don't let up."

Robin exchanged determined looks with Jake and Alex. They were ready to finish what they had started.

The halftime whistle had barely faded from memory when the opposition stormed onto the pitch with renewed vigour. It was clear that they had regrouped and adjusted their strategy. Robin stood in the midfield, feeling the weight of the lead on his shoulders as the referee blew the whistle for the second half to begin.

The opposition wasted no time asserting themselves. Within minutes, their striker broke through the defensive line, darting into space. A precise pass from their midfield found him in the box, and with a clinical touch, he slotted the ball past Tommy.

3-1.

Robin's heart sank as the crowd erupted, the cheers of the opposition's fans filling the air. He looked back at Tommy, who clenched his fists in frustration but gave a nod of reassurance. "Keep your heads up, guys," Robin called out, rallying his teammates. "We've got this. Just stay compact."

But before they could regroup, disaster struck again. A quick counterattack down the left flank caught the defence off guard. The opposition's winger sent a low cross into the box, and their forward tapped it in at close range.

3-2.

Robin's stomach churned. The once-commanding lead was now just a single goal. He glanced at Jake and Alex, who were exchanging worried looks. "We need to stay calm," Robin said firmly. "Let's focus on what we've practised."

The opposition, sensing their momentum, pushed harder. They earned a corner after a deflected shot went wide. Robin jogged back into the box, his pulse quickening as he took his position. The players lined up, ready to defend.

Coach's words echoed in Robin's mind: *Stay tight. Mark your man. No room for errors.*

The ball soared into the air, curling toward the near post. Alex, marking their tallest player, leapt high, barely getting a touch. The ball deflected to the far post, where another attacker was lurking. Before he could get a clean shot, Ollie lunged in, blocking the ball with his body. It ricocheted out to Robin, who wasted no time clearing it upfield.

"Well done, Ollie!" Robin shouted, his voice strained with adrenaline.

Ollie gave him a quick thumbs-up, his face red with effort. "Let's keep them out!"

Minutes later, a clumsy challenge from Jake just outside the box led to a free kick. Robin and his teammates formed a tense wall as Tommy crouched low, his eyes locked on the ball. The opposition's captain stood over it, his posture radiating confidence.

Robin could hear Tommy's steady voice behind him. "Hold the line. Don't flinch."

The whistle blew, and the captain struck the ball with precision. It curled over the wall, dipping toward the top corner. Tommy sprang into action, diving at full stretch. His fingertips grazed the ball, pushing it onto the post.

The ball rebounded into the box, chaos ensuing as players scrambled for it. Robin rushed back, sliding in to clear the ball before an attacker could pounce. The crowd erupted in applause, the tension on the pitch palpable.

"That was incredible, Tommy!" Robin shouted, helping his teammate to his feet.

Tommy grinned, his face flushed. "Just doing my job."

The opposition wasn't done yet. They switched their focus to the flanks, trying to exploit the space on the wings. Their right winger, quick and skilful, danced past Alex and sent a dangerous cross into the box. Robin sprinted back, heart pounding, and managed to intercept the ball mid-air with a header.

"Nice one, Robin!" Jake called as he chased the loose ball to clear it further.

But the winger came again, this time cutting inside. He unleashed a powerful shot aimed at the bottom corner. Tommy dived, palming the ball away, and Alex was there to blast it upfield. The defenders exchanged quick, determined nods, the unspoken promise to hold their line stronger than ever.

The clock ticked down, the game entering its final moments. The opposition, desperate for an equaliser, launched another attack. In a tangle of legs and bodies inside the box, Ollie accidentally tripped their striker. The referee's whistle pierced the air, his arm pointing to the penalty spot.

Robin's stomach dropped. He could see Ollie's face pale with guilt. "Sorry, guys," Ollie muttered, his voice barely audible.

Tommy stepped forward, his expression calm despite the tension radiating from the crowd. He adjusted his gloves, planting himself firmly on the line.

The opposition's striker placed the ball, taking a few steps back. The stadium fell into a tense silence as he began his run-up. The shot was low and hard, aimed at the bottom left corner. Tommy guessed right, diving with perfect timing. His outstretched hand smothered the ball, and he quickly leapt on top of it, securing it in his grasp.

The stadium erupted into cheers, the tension breaking like a wave. Robin sprinted over, pulling Tommy to his feet. "You're a legend!" he shouted, grinning from ear to ear.

Tommy shrugged, his smile modest. "Just doing my job."

As the referee blew the final whistle, Robin felt a surge of relief and pride. They had held on, weathering wave after wave of attacks, and emerged victorious. The players embraced, their camaraderie stronger than ever.

Coach Thompson gathered them in a huddle on the pitch. "This was your best game yet," he said, his voice filled with pride. "You stayed resilient, you stayed compact, and you fought for each other. That's what this season has been about."

Robin looked around at his teammates, their faces shining with sweat and joy. It wasn't just a victory; it was proof of how far they had come.

Mental Resilience in Defence

Resilience is built not in victory, but in the lessons of every battle fought.

The sun was setting, casting a warm orange hue over the local park where the team had gathered for their last meeting of the season. Coach Thompson had organised a relaxed picnic for the players, their families, and a few close supporters. The tables were laden with food, and the mood was lighthearted, the tension of the games replaced with camaraderie and laughter.

Robin sat with Jake, Ollie, Alex, and Tommy, sharing stories about the season's most memorable moments.

"Remember when Alex went in for that sliding tackle and nearly knocked himself over?" Jake said, laughing as he shoved a piece of bread into his mouth.

Alex groaned but couldn't help grinning. "Hey, at least I stopped the attack!"

Ollie leaned in. "And Tommy's penalty save in the last game? I've never seen anything like it."

Tommy shrugged, trying to look modest. "Just doing my job."

Robin smiled, enjoying the moment. They weren't just teammates anymore; they were friends who had shared victories, defeats, and lessons both on and off the pitch.

As the evening drew on, Coach Thompson called everyone together, his voice carrying over the gentle chatter. The players and families gathered around, forming a semicircle on the grass.

"First," Coach began, looking around at the group, "I want to thank all of you. Parents, players, and supporters—you've all played a part in making this season special. What we've achieved isn't just about the games we've played but about the lessons we've learned and the team we've become."

He paused, letting his words sink in. Robin felt a swell of pride, knowing how far they had come since the start of the season.

"This season, we've focused on defence," Coach continued. "Not just as a tactic but as a mindset. Defence isn't just about stopping goals—it's about resilience, discipline, and mental toughness. It's about staying strong when the pressure is on, holding your ground when things don't go your way, and supporting each other no matter what."

He turned to Alex. "Alex, your sliding tackle in the rival game might not have been perfect, but you showed courage. And more importantly, you owned up to it and made sure to learn from it."

Alex nodded, his expression serious.

"And Tommy," Coach said, smiling, "your penalty save wasn't just skill—it was mental resilience. You stayed calm under pressure, trusted yourself, and delivered when it mattered most."

Tommy blushed but grinned. "Thanks, Coach."

Coach addressed the whole team. "Mental resilience is the foundation of great defence. It's what allows you to bounce back after a mistake, stay focused when the odds are against you, and push through the toughest moments. And that's not just true in soccer—it's true in life."

Coach Thompson glanced at the horizon, the sun dipping below the trees. "This season has been about more than soccer. It's been about growth. Each of you has grown, not just as a player but as an individual. And that's something you should be proud of."

He looked at Robin and his teammates. "Next season, we'll face new challenges. But remember this season. Remember what you've learned about resilience, teamwork, and discipline. Those lessons will carry you forward, both on and off the pitch."

The players erupted into applause, cheering for their coach and for each other. The families joined in, their pride evident in their smiles.

As the gathering wound down, Robin stood with his friends, looking out at the field where they had trained, struggled, and triumphed together.

"This season was incredible," Robin said, his voice filled with emotion. "I've learned so much, not just about soccer but about myself."

Ollie grinned. "And we've all got you to thank for being our anchor, mate."

"Yeah," Jake added, clapping Robin on the back. "You're like the glue that keeps us together."

Robin smiled, humbled by their words. "It's all of us. We're a team, and that's what made this season special."

As the group dispersed, heading home with their families, Robin took one last look at the field. He knew this wasn't the end—just the beginning of another chapter. With everything he had learned and the bonds he had built, he felt ready for whatever challenges lay ahead.

And with that thought, Robin turned and walked away, the future wide open and filled with possibility.

This marks the close of another chapter in Robin's journey. The lessons learned, both in soccer and in life, will shape him and his teammates as they grow. A reminder that soccer is more than just a game—it's a metaphor for resilience, teamwork, and perseverance.

THE END

until the next challange
begins...

Afterword

Thank you for joining Robin and his team on this exciting journey through *On the Pitch: Mastering the Defence*. Writing this book has been a wonderful exploration of the discipline, determination, and resilience required to defend both on the pitch and in life. Each chapter was carefully crafted to emphasise the importance of defensive skills while also showcasing the strength of character that comes from standing firm in the face of challenges.

In this fourth book of the series, I wanted to highlight how defence is more than just preventing goals—it's about teamwork, strategy, and a relentless commitment to protecting what matters most. Robin's story reminds us that while defenders may not always get the spotlight, their role is vital, and their efforts often make the difference between success and failure. My hope is that Robin's journey inspires you to embrace the value of grit and determination in all areas of life and to see the strength in standing your ground for the team and the goals you believe in.

It has been an honour to share this defensive season with you, and I'm excited for what lies ahead in Robin's journey. Remember, whether you're defending on the pitch or standing up for something you believe in, resilience, focus, and teamwork will always make a difference.

Thank you for reading and being part of this story. Keep standing tall, keep believing, and always play with heart and passion.

Toby Rivers

Printed in Great Britain
by Amazon